WHISPER

TWENTY-ONE DESIGNS BY KIM HARGREAVES

CREDITS

DESIGNS & STYLING
Kim Hargreaves

EDITOR
Kathleen Hargreaves

MODEL
Kristie Stubley

HAIR & MAKE-UP
Diana Fisher

PHOTOGRAPHY & EDITORIAL DESIGN
Graham Watts

LAYOUTS
Angela Lin

PATTERNS
Sue Whiting & Trisha McKenzie

First published in 2011 by Kim Hargreaves
Intake Cottage, 26 Underbank Old Road, Holmfirth
West Yorkshire, HD9 1EA, England

British Library Cataloguing in Publication Data
A catalogue record for this book is available from the British Library

ISBN-10   1-906487-10-2
ISBN-13   978-1-906487-10-2

CONTENTS

Minimal simplicity merges with edgy style,
whilst shades of black & white offer a sharp
contrast to pretty feminine designs

L

CHRISTINA | *Cardigan with pretty textured stripes*

SALICE | *Sharp crochet jacket with side vents*

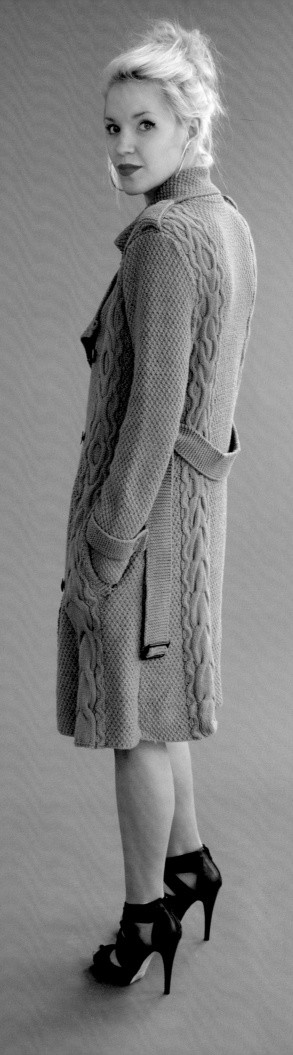

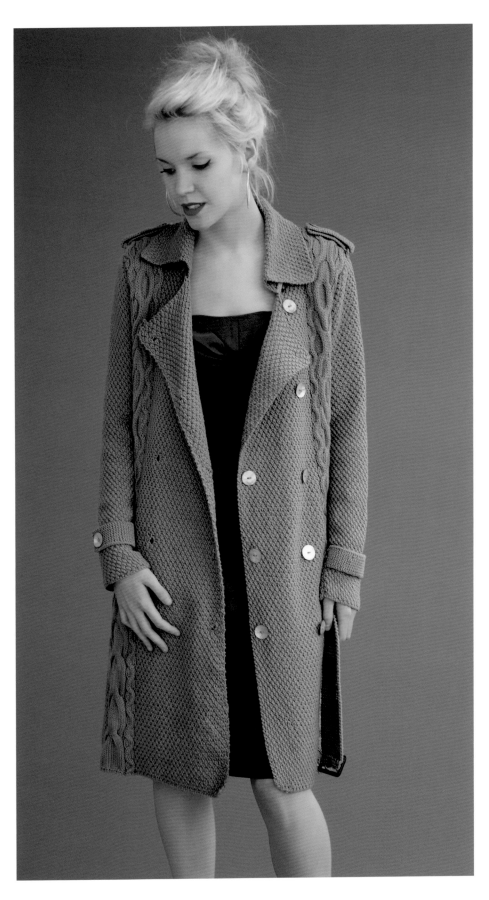

TORA | *Classic trench coat with cable & epaulet details*

RITA | *Neat cardigan with lace trims & ribbon tie*

DANIELA | *Cabled & garter stitch belted cardigan*

CAMEO | *Ribbed jacket with deep raglans*

CAMELLIA | *Close-fitting hat with pretty detail*

GABRIELA | *Delicate cropped cabled cardigan*

EBONY | *Skimming tunic worked in an open stitch*

CAMELLIA | *Close-fitting hat with pretty detail*

EBONY | *Skimming tunic worked in an open stitch*

JOLE | *Slightly slouchy textured hat*

BEL | *A neat cropped cardigan*

MARSHA | *Lace edged garter stitch cardigan*

PATTERNS

THE

THE PATTERNS

EDDA
Chic edge to edge jacket

Recommendation
Suitable for the knitter with a little experience
Please see pages 18 & 19 for photographs.

	XS	S	M	L	XL	XXL	
To fit	**81**	**86**	**91**	**97**	**102**	**109**	cm
bust	32	34	36	38	40	43	in

Rowan All Seasons Cotton
6	6	7	7	8	9	x 50gm

Photographed in Black

Needles
1 pair 4mm (no 8) (US 6) needles
1 pair 4½mm (no 7) (US 7) needles
Cable needle

Tension
16 sts and 28 rows to 10 cm measured over
pattern using 4½mm (US 7) needles.

BACK
Cast on 55 (59: 63: 67: 71: 77) sts using
4½mm (US 7) needles.
Row 1 (RS): K1 (3: 5: 7: 2: 5), (yfrn, P2tog,
K5) 0 (0: 0: 0: 1: 1) times, *yfrn, P2tog, K5,
yfrn, P2tog*, K1, inc once in each of next 3 sts,
K1, rep from * to * once more, K7, rep from *
to * once more, K1, inc once in each of next
3 sts, K1, rep from * to * once more, (K5, yfrn,
P2tog) 0 (0: 0: 0: 1: 1) times, K1 (3: 5: 7: 2: 5).
61 (65: 69: 73: 77: 83) sts.
Now work in patt as folls:
Row 1 (WS): K1 (3: 5: 7: 2: 5), (yfrn, P2tog,
K5) 0 (0: 0: 0: 1: 1) times, *yfrn, P2tog, K5,
yfrn, P2tog*, P8, rep from * to * once more, K7,
rep from * to * once more, P8, rep from * to *
once more, (K5, yfrn, P2tog) 0 (0: 0: 0: 1: 1)
times, K1 (3: 5: 7: 2: 5).
Row 2: K1 (3: 5: 7: 2: 5), (yfrn, P2tog, K5)
0 (0: 0: 0: 1: 1) times, *yfrn, P2tog, K5, yfrn,
P2tog*, K8, rep from * to * once more, K7, rep
from * to * once more, K8, rep from * to * once
more, (K5, yfrn, P2tog) 0 (0: 0: 0: 1: 1) times,
K1 (3: 5: 7: 2: 5).
Rows 3 to 8: As rows 1 and 2, 3 times.
Row 9: As row 1.
Row 10: K1 (3: 5: 7: 2: 5), (yfrn, P2tog, K5)
0 (0: 0: 0: 1: 1) times, *yfrn, P2tog, K5, yfrn,
P2tog*, C8B, rep from * to * once more, K7,
rep from * to * once more, C8F, rep from * to
* once more, (K5, yfrn, P2tog) 0 (0: 0: 0: 1: 1)
times, K1 (3: 5: 7: 2: 5).
Rows 11 and 12: As rows 1 and 2.
These 12 rows form patt.
Keeping patt correct, dec 1 st at each end of 2nd
and foll 10th row. 57 (61: 65: 69: 73: 79) sts.
Work 13 rows, ending with a WS row.
Inc 1 st at each end of next and 3 foll 14th
rows, taking inc sts into patt.
65 (69: 73: 77: 81: 87) sts.
Cont straight until back measures 32 (32: 33:
33: 33: 33) cm, ending with a WS row.
Shape armholes
Keeping patt correct, cast off 3 (4: 4: 5: 5: 6) sts
at beg of next 2 rows. 59 (61: 65: 67: 71: 75) sts.
Dec 1 st at each end of next 3 (3: 3: 3: 3: 5)
rows, then on foll 1 (1: 2: 2: 3: 2) alt rows, then
on foll 4th row. 49 (51: 53: 55: 57: 59) sts.
Cont straight until armhole measures 17 (18:
18: 19: 20: 21) cm, ending with a WS row.

Shape shoulders and back neck
Cast off 5 (5: 5: 5: 5: 6) sts at beg of next
2 rows. 39 (41: 43: 45: 47: 47) sts.
Next row (RS): Cast off 5 (5: 5: 5: 5: 6)
sts, patt until there are 8 (8: 9: 9: 10: 9)
sts on right needle and turn, leaving rem
sts on a holder.
Work each side of neck separately.
Cast off 4 sts at beg of next row.
Cast off rem 4 (4: 5: 5: 6: 5) sts.
With RS facing, rejoin yarn to rem sts, cast off
centre 13 (15: 15: 17: 17: 17) sts, patt to end.
Complete to match first side, reversing
shapings.

LEFT FRONT
Cast on 32 (34: 36: 38: 40: 43) sts using
4½mm (US 7) needles.
Row 1 (RS): K1 (3: 5: 7: 2: 5), (yfrn, P2tog,
K5) 0 (0: 0: 0: 1: 1) times, *yfrn, P2tog, K5,
yfrn, P2tog*, K1, inc once in each of next 3 sts,
K1, rep from * to * once more, K8.
35 (37: 39: 41: 43: 46) sts.
Now work in patt as folls:
Row 1 (WS): K8, *yfrn, P2tog, K5, yfrn, P2tog*,
P8, rep from * to * once more, (K5, yfrn, P2tog)
0 (0: 0: 0: 1: 1) times, K1 (3: 5: 7: 2: 5).
Row 2: K1 (3: 5: 7: 2: 5), (yfrn, P2tog, K5)
0 (0: 0: 0: 1: 1) times, *yfrn, P2tog, K5, yfrn,
P2tog*, K8, rep from * to * once more, K8.
Rows 3 to 8: As rows 1 and 2, 3 times.
Row 9: As row 1.
Row 10: K1 (3: 5: 7: 2: 5), (yfrn, P2tog, K5)
0 (0: 0: 0: 1: 1) times, *yfrn, P2tog, K5, yfrn,
P2tog*, C8B, rep from * to * once more, K8.
Rows 11 and 12: As rows 1 and 2.
These 12 rows form patt.
Keeping patt correct, dec 1 st at beg of 2nd
and foll 10th row. 33 (35: 37: 39: 41: 44) sts.
Work 13 rows, ending with a WS row.
Inc 1 st at beg of next and 3 foll 14th rows,
taking inc sts into patt.
37 (39: 41: 43: 45: 48) sts.
Cont straight until left front matches back to
start of armhole shaping, ending with a WS row.
Shape armhole
Keeping patt correct, cast off 3 (4: 4: 5: 5: 6)
sts at beg of next row.
34 (35: 37: 38: 40: 42) sts.
Work 1 row.

Dec 1 st at armhole edge of next 3 (3: 3: 3: 3: 5) rows, then on foll 1 (1: 2: 2: 3: 2) alt rows, then on foll 4th row.
29 (30: 31: 32: 33: 34) sts.
Cont straight until 14 (14: 14: 16: 16: 16) rows less have been worked than on back to start of shoulder shaping, ending with a WS row.

Shape front neck
Next row (RS): Patt 19 (19: 20: 21: 22: 23) sts and turn, leaving rem 10 (11: 11: 11: 11: 11) sts on a holder.
Keeping patt correct, dec 1 st at neck edge of next 2 rows, then on foll 2 (2: 2: 3: 3: 3) alt rows, then on foll 4th row.
14 (14: 15: 15: 16: 17) sts.
Work 3 rows, ending with a WS row.

Shape shoulder
Cast off 5 (5: 5: 5: 5: 6) sts at beg of next and foll alt row.
Work 1 row.
Cast off rem 4 (4: 5: 5: 6: 5) sts.

RIGHT FRONT
Cast on 32 (34: 36: 38: 40: 43) sts using 4½mm (US 7) needles.
Row 1 (RS): K8, *yfrn, P2tog, K5, yfrn, P2tog*, K1, inc once in each of next 3 sts, K1, rep from * to * once more, (K5, yfrn, P2tog) 0 (0: 0: 0: 1: 1) times, K1 (3: 5: 7: 2: 5).
35 (37: 39: 41: 43: 46) sts.
Now work in patt as folls:
Row 1 (WS): K1 (3: 5: 7: 2: 5), (yfrn, P2tog, K5) 0 (0: 0: 0: 1: 1) times, *yfrn, P2tog, K5, yfrn, P2tog*, P8, rep from * to * once more, K8.
Row 2: K8, *yfrn, P2tog, K5, yfrn, P2tog*, K8, rep from * to * once more, (K5, yfrn, P2tog) 0 (0: 0: 0: 1: 1) times, K1 (3: 5: 7: 2: 5).
Rows 3 to 8: As rows 1 and 2, 3 times.
Row 9: As row 1.
Row 10: K8, *yfrn, P2tog, K5, yfrn, P2tog*, C8F, rep from * to * once more, (K5, yfrn, P2tog) 0 (0: 0: 0: 1: 1) times, K1 (3: 5: 7: 2: 5).
Rows 11 and 12: As rows 1 and 2.
These 12 rows form patt.
Keeping patt correct, dec 1 st at end of 2nd and foll 10th row.
33 (35: 37: 39: 41: 44) sts.
Complete to match left front, reversing shapings and working first row of neck shaping as folls:

Shape front neck
Next row (RS): Patt 10 (11: 11: 11: 11: 11) sts and slip these sts onto a holder, patt to end.
19 (19: 20: 21: 22: 23) sts.

SLEEVES (both alike)
Cast on 43 (45: 47: 49: 51: 53) sts using 4½mm (US 7) needles.
Row 1 (RS): K3 (4: 5: 6: 7: 8), yfrn, P2tog, (K5, yfrn, P2tog) 5 times, K3 (4: 5: 6: 7: 8).
Row 2: As row 1.
These 2 rows form patt.
Cont in patt, inc 1 st at each end of 3rd and foll 4th (4th: 4th: 4th: 6th: 6th) row, taking inc sts into g st.
47 (49: 51: 53: 55: 57) sts.
Cont straight until sleeve measures 4 (4: 5: 5: 6: 6) cm, ending with a WS row.

Shape top
Keeping patt correct, cast off 3 (4: 4: 5: 5: 6) sts at beg of next 2 rows.
41 (41: 43: 43: 45: 45) sts.
Dec 1 st at each end of next 3 rows, then on foll alt row, then on foll 4th row, then on 2 foll 6th rows.
27 (27: 29: 29: 31: 31) sts.
Work 3 rows, ending with a WS row.

Size XXL only
Dec 1 st at each end of next row. 29 sts.
Work 3 rows, ending with a WS row.

All sizes
Dec 1 st at each end of next and foll 1 (3: 2: 4: 5: 4) alt rows, then on foll 5 (3: 5: 3: 3: 3) rows, ending with a WS row.
Cast off rem 13 sts.

MAKING UP
Press all pieces with a warm iron over a damp cloth.
Join both shoulder seams using back stitch or mattress stitch if preferred.

Neckband
With RS facing and using 4mm (US 6) needles, slip 10 (11: 11: 11: 11: 11) sts from right front holder onto right needle, rejoin yarn and pick up and knit 17 (17: 17: 19: 19: 19) sts up right side of neck, 21 (23: 23: 25: 25: 25) sts from back, and 17 (17: 17: 19: 19: 19) sts down left side of neck, then patt across 10 (11: 11: 11: 11: 11) sts on left front holder.
75 (79: 79: 85: 85: 85) sts.
Work in g st for 2 rows, ending with a RS row.
Cast off knitwise (on **WS**).
Join side seams. Join sleeve seams. Insert sleeves.

38.5 (41: 43.5: 46: 48.5: 52) cm
15 (16: 17: 18: 19: 20½) in

49 (50: 51: 52: 53: 54) cm
19¼ (19¾: 20: 20½: 21: 21¼) in

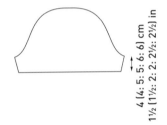

4 (4: 5: 5: 6: 6) cm
1½ (1½: 2: 2: 2½: 2½) in

SOPHIA
Elegant sweater with buttoned neck-line

Recommendation
Suitable for the knitter with a little experience
Please see pages 20 & 21 for photographs.

	XS	S	M	L	XL	XXL	
To fit	**81**	**86**	**91**	**97**	**102**	**109**	cm
bust	32	34	36	38	40	43	in

Rowan Cotton Glace
| | 7 | 7 | 8 | 8 | 9 | 10 | x 50gm |

Photographed in Black

Needles
1 pair 2¾mm (no 12) (US 2) needles
1 pair 3mm (no 11) (US 2/3) needles
1 pair 3¼mm (no 10) (US 3) needles
2¾mm (no 12) (US 2) circular needle

Buttons – 5 (6: 6: 6: 6: 6)

Tension
23 sts and 32 rows to 10 cm measured over
stocking stitch using 3¼mm (US 3) needles.

BACK
Cast on 91 (97: 103: 109: 115: 123) sts
using 2¾mm (US 2) needles.
Work in g st for 10 rows, ending with a WS row.
Change to 3¼mm (US 3) needles.
Now work in patt as folls:
Beg with a K row, work in st st for 9 rows, dec 1 st
at each end of 7th of these rows and ending with
a **RS** row. 89 (95: 101: 107: 113: 121) sts.
Beg with a K row, work in rev st st for 5 rows, dec
1 st at each end of 4th of these rows and ending
with a WS row. 87 (93: 99: 105: 111: 119) sts.
Beg with a K row, work in st st for 9 rows, dec 1
st at each end of 5th of these rows and ending
with a **RS** row. 85 (91: 97: 103: 109: 117) sts.
Row 24 (WS): Knit.
Last 24 rows form patt and beg side seam
shaping.
Cont in patt, dec 1 st at each end of next
and foll 6th row. 81 (87: 93: 99: 105: 113) sts.
Work 17 rows, ending with a WS row.
Inc 1 st at each end of next and 5 foll 14th
rows. 93 (99: 105: 111: 117: 125) sts.
Work 9 rows, ending after 8 rows in st st
and with a WS row.
(Back should measure approx 42 cm)
Shape raglan armholes
Change to 3mm (US 2/3) needles.
Now working in g st throughout, cont as folls:
Cast off 6 sts at beg of next 2 rows.
81 (87: 93: 99: 105: 113) sts.**
Work 4 (4: 0: 0: 0: 0) rows, ending with
a WS row.
Next row (RS): K3, K2tog, K to last 5 sts,
K2tog tbl, K3.
Working all decreases as set by last row, dec 1
st at each end of 2 (-: 4: 6: 10: 16) foll 6th (-:
alt: alt: alt: alt) rows, then on 8 (12: 11: 11: 10:
8) foll 4th rows. 59 (61: 61: 63: 63: 63) sts.
Work 3 rows, ending with a WS row.
Cast off.

FRONT
Work as given for back to **.
Divide for front opening
Next row (RS): (K3, K2tog) 0 (0: 0: 1: 1: 1)
times, K38 (41: 39: 42: 45: 49) and slip these
38 (41: 43: 46: 49: 53) sts onto a holder, K to
last 0 (0: 5: 5: 5: 5) sts, (K2tog tbl, K3) 0 (0: 1:
1: 1: 1) times. 43 (46: 48: 51: 54: 58) sts.

Work each side of neck separately.
Next row (WS): Knit.
Sizes S, M and L only
Next row (buttonhole row) (RS): K1, K2tog,
yfwd (to make first buttonhole), K2, yfwd,
K2tog (to form eyelet line defining front band),
K to last - (0: 5: 5: -: -) sts, (K2tog tbl, K3) - (0:
1: 1: -: -) times. - (46: 47: 50: -: -) sts.
Last 2 rows set the sts - front band 5 sts
defined by a line of eyelet holes and all
other sts in g st.
Sizes XS, XL and XXL only
Next row (RS): K5, yfwd, K2tog (to form eyelet
line defining front band), K to last 0 (-: -: -: 5:
5) sts, (K2tog tbl, K3) 0 (-: -: -: 1: 1) times.
43 (-: -: -: 53: 57) sts.
Last 2 rows set the sts - front band 5 sts
defined by a line of eyelet holes and all other
sts in g st.
Cont as set, dec 1 st at raglan armhole edge of
2nd (-: -: -: 2nd: 2nd) and foll 0 (-: -: -: 0: 1) alt
row. 42 (-: -: -: 52: 55) sts.
Work 1 row, ending with a WS row.
Next row (buttonhole row) (RS): K1, K2tog,
yfwd (to make first buttonhole), K2, yfwd,
K2tog (for eyelet line), K to last 0 (-: -: -: 5: 5)
sts, (K2tog tbl, K3) 0 (-: -: -: 1: 1) times. 42 (-:
-: -: 51: 54) sts.
All sizes
Making a further 3 (4: 4: 4: 4: 4) buttonholes
as set by last row on every foll 8th row and
noting that no further reference will be made
to buttonholes, cont as folls:
Dec 1 st at raglan armhole edge of 4th (2nd:
2nd: 2nd: 2nd: 2nd) and 1 (-: 2: 4: 6: 11) foll
6th (-: alt: alt: alt: alt) rows, then on 4 (8: 7: 6:
5: 3) foll 4th rows.
36 (37: 37: 39: 39: 39) sts.
Work 3 rows, ending with a WS row.
Shape front neck
Next row (RS): Patt 25 (26: 26: 25: 25: 25)
sts and slip these sts onto another holder,
K to last 5 sts, K2tog tbl, K3.
10 (10: 10: 13: 13: 13) sts.
Dec 1 st at neck edge of next 6 rows **and at
same time** dec 1 st at raglan armhole edge
of 4th row. 3 (3: 3: 6: 6: 6) sts.
Sizes L, XL and XXL only
Work 1 row, ending with a WS row.
Next row (RS): K3, K3tog tbl. 4 sts.

Work 1 row.
Dec 1 st at neck edge of next row. 3 sts.
All sizes
Work 1 row, ending with a WS row.
Next row (RS): K3tog.
Next row: K1 and fasten off.
With WS facing, rejoin yarn to rem sts, cast on
5 sts, K to end. 43 (46: 48: 51: 54: 58) sts.
Next row (RS): (K3, K2tog) 0 (0: 1: 1: 1: 1)
times, K to last 7 sts, K2tog, yfwd (to form
eyelet line defining front band), K5.
Complete to match first side, reversing
shapings and working first row of neck shaping
as folls:
Shape front neck
Next row (RS): K3, K2tog, K6 (6: 6: 9: 9: 9)
and turn, leaving rem 25 (26: 26: 25: 25: 25)
sts on a holder. 10 (10: 10: 13: 13: 13) sts.

SLEEVES (both alike)
Cast on 129 (129: 135: 141: 141: 153) sts
using 2¾mm (US 2) needles.
Row 1 (RS): K3, *cast off 3 sts, K until there are
3 sts on right needle after cast-off, rep from *
to end. 66 (66: 69: 72: 72: 78) sts.
Now working in g st throughout, cont as folls:
Work 7 rows, dec (inc: -: dec: inc: dec) 1 (1:
-: 1: 1: 1) st at beg of first of these rows and
ending with a WS row.
65 (67: 69: 71: 73: 77) sts.
Change to 3mm (US 2/3) needles.
Shape raglan
Cast off 6 sts at beg of next 2 rows.
53 (55: 57: 59: 61: 65) sts.
Working all raglan decreases in same way as
raglan armhole decreases, dec 1 st at each end
of 7th (5th: 3rd: 3rd: 3rd: 3rd) and 0 (0: 2: 3:
4: 8) foll 4th rows, then on 6 (7: 6: 6: 6: 4) foll
6th rows. 39 sts.
Work 3 rows, ending with a WS row.
Left sleeve only
Work 1 row.
Cast off 9 sts at beg of next and foll 2 alt rows,
ending with a WS row, **and at same time** dec
1 st at beg of 2nd row.
Right sleeve only
Cast off 9 sts at beg of next and foll 2 alt rows
and at same time dec 1 st at end of 3rd row.
Work 1 row, ending with a WS row.
Both sleeves
Cast off rem 11 sts.

MAKING UP
Press all pieces with a warm iron over a damp
cloth.
Join all raglan seams using back stitch or
mattress stitch if preferred.

Neckband
With RS facing and using 2¾mm (US 2)
circular needle, slip 25 (26: 26: 25: 25: 25) sts
from right front holder onto right needle, rejoin
yarn and pick up and knit 10 (10: 10: 14: 14:
14) sts up right side of neck, 36 sts from top
of right sleeve placing markers either side of
these sts and between centre 2 sts, 57 (59: 59:
61: 61: 61) sts from back, 36 sts from top of
left sleeve placing markers either side of these
sts and between centre 2 sts, and 10 (10: 10:
14: 14: 14) sts down left side of neck, then
patt across 25 (26: 26: 25: 25: 25) sts on left
front holder.
199 (203: 203: 211: 211: 211) sts, 6 markers
in total.
Keeping eyelet lines correct as set and working
all other sts in g st, work 1 row, ending with
a WS row.
Row 2 (buttonhole row) (RS): K1, K2tog,
yfwd (to make last buttonhole), *patt to within
4 sts of marker, K2tog tbl, K4 (marker is at
centre of these 4 sts), K2tog, rep from * 5
times more, patt to end.
187 (191: 191: 199: 199: 199) sts.
Work 3 rows.
Row 6 (RS): *Patt to within 4 sts of marker,
K2tog tbl, K4 (marker is at centre of these
4 sts), K2tog, rep from * 5 times more, patt
to end. 175 (179: 179: 187: 187: 187) sts.
Work 2 rows, ending with a **RS** row.
Cast off knitwise (on **WS**).
Join side and sleeve seams. At base of front
opening, sew cast-on edge of left side of front
in place behind right side of front.
Sew on buttons.

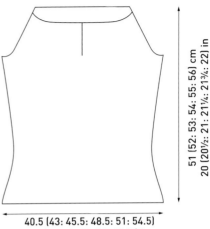

51 (52: 53: 54: 55: 56) cm
20 (20½: 21: 21¼: 21¾: 22) in

40.5 (43: 45.5: 48.5: 51: 54.5)
16 (17: 18: 19: 20: 21 ½) in

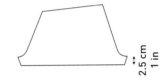

2.5 cm
1 in

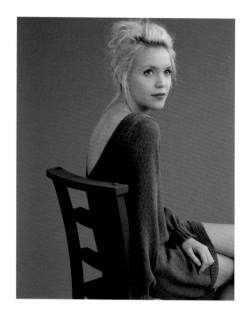

Recommendation

Suitable for the knitter with a little experience
Please see pages 22 & 23 for photographs.

	XS	S	M	L	XL	XXL	
To fit	**81**	**86**	**91**	**97**	**102**	**109**	cm
bust	32	34	36	38	40	43	in

Rowan Pima Cotton

| | 10 | 11 | 12 | 13 | 14 | 15 x 50gm |

Photographed in Badger

Needles

1 pair 3¼mm (no 10) (US 3) needles
1 pair 3¾mm (no 9) (US 5) needles

Tension

23 sts and 30 rows to 10 cm measured over
stocking stitch using 3¾mm (US 5) needles.

SHEER
Reversible A-line tunic with full sleeves

BACK

Cast on 114 (120: 126: 132: 138: 148) sts
using 3¼mm (US 3) needles.
Work in g st for 10 rows, ending with
a WS row.
Row 11 (RS): K1, *K2tog, yfwd, rep from * to
last st, K1.
Work in g st for 5 rows, ending with a WS row.
Row 17: As row 11.
Work in g st for 3 rows, ending with a WS row.
Change to 3¾mm (US 5) needles.
Beg with a K row, work in st st for 4 rows,
ending with a WS row.
Next row (dec) (RS): K3, K2tog, K to last
5 sts, K2tog tbl, K3.
Working all side seam decreases as set by last
row, dec 1 st at each end of 16th and every foll
16th row until 98 (104: 110: 116: 122: 132)
sts rem.
Cont straight until back measures 56 (56: 57:
57: 57: 57) cm, ending with a WS row.
Shape armholes
Cast off 4 (4: 5: 5: 6: 6) sts at beg of next
2 rows. 90 (96: 100: 106: 110: 120) sts.
Dec 1 st at each end of next 5 (5: 7: 7: 9: 9)
rows, then on foll 3 (5: 4: 6: 5: 8) alt rows, then
on foll 4th row. 72 (74: 76: 78: 80: 84) sts.
Cont straight until armhole measures 14.5
(15.5: 15.5: 16.5: 17.5: 18.5) cm, ending
with a WS row.
Shape back neck
Next row (RS): K17 (17: 18: 18: 19: 21) and
turn, leaving rem sts on a holder.
Work each side of neck separately.
Dec 1 st at neck edge of next 6 rows, then on
foll 2 alt rows. 9 (9: 10: 10: 11: 13) sts.
Work 1 row, ending with a WS row.
Shape shoulder
Cast off 4 (4: 5: 5: 5: 6) sts at beg of next row.
Work 1 row.
Cast off rem 5 (5: 5: 5: 6: 7) sts.
With RS facing, rejoin yarn to rem sts, cast off
centre 38 (40: 40: 42: 42: 42) sts, K to end.
Complete to match first side, reversing
shapings.

FRONT

Work as given for back until 12 rows less have
been worked than on back to start of armhole
shaping, ending with a WS row.

Shape front neck
Next row (RS): K42 (44: 47: 49: 52: 57) and
turn, leaving rem sts on a holder.
Work each side of neck separately.
Cast off 3 sts at beg of next row.
39 (41: 44: 46: 49: 54) sts.
Dec 1 st at neck edge of next 5 rows, then on
foll 2 alt rows. 32 (34: 37: 39: 42: 47) sts.
Work 1 row, ending with a WS row.
Shape armhole
Cast off 4 (4: 5: 5: 6: 6) sts at beg and dec 1 st
at end of next row. 27 (29: 31: 33: 35: 40) sts.
Work 1 row.
Dec 1 st at neck edge of next and foll alt row
(place marker on this last dec), then on 4 foll
4th rows, then on foll 6th row, then on foll 8th
row, then on foll 10th row **and at same time**
dec 1 st at armhole edge of next 5 (5: 7: 7: 9:
9) rows, then on foll 3 (5: 4: 6: 5: 8) alt rows,
then on foll 4th row. 9 (9: 10: 10: 11: 13) sts.
Cont straight until front matches back to start
of shoulder shaping, ending with a WS row.
Shape shoulder
Cast off 4 (4: 5: 5: 5: 6) sts at beg of next row.
Work 1 row.
Cast off rem 5 (5: 5: 5: 6: 7) sts.
With RS facing, rejoin yarn to rem sts, cast
off centre 14 (16: 16: 18: 18: 18) sts placing
markers at both ends of these sts, K to end.
Complete to match first side, reversing shapings.

SLEEVES (both alike)
Main section

Cast on 94 (96: 98: 100: 104: 106) sts using
3¾mm (US 5) needles.
Beg with a K row and working all decreases in
same way as side seam decreases, work in st
st, shaping sides by dec 1 st at each end of 9th
and 9 foll 6th rows, then on foll 8th row, then
on foll 12th row. 70 (72: 74: 76: 80: 82) sts.
Cont straight until main section measures 34
(35: 36: 37: 38: 39) cm, ending with a WS row.
Shape top
Cast off 4 (4: 5: 5: 6: 6) sts at beg of next
2 rows. 62 (64: 64: 66: 68: 70) sts.
Dec 1 st at each end of next 3 rows, then on
foll alt row, then on foll 4th row, then on foll 6th
row, then on 3 foll 4th rows.
44 (46: 48: 48: 50: 52) sts.
Work 1 row, ending with a WS row.

Dec 1 st at each end of next and every foll alt row to 38 sts, then on foll 5 rows, ending with a WS row.
Cast off rem 28 sts.

Cuff

With RS facing and using 3¼mm (US 3) needles, pick up and knit 96 (96: 96: 96: 104: 104) sts evenly along cast-on edge of main section.

Next row (WS): K2, *(P2tog) twice, (K2tog) twice, rep from * to last 6 sts, (P2tog) twice, K2.
50 (50: 50: 50: 54: 54) sts.

Next row: P2, *K2, P2, rep from * to end.

Next row: K2, *P2, K2, rep from * to end.
Last 2 rows form rib.
Cont in rib until cuff measures 7 cm from pick-up row, ending with a WS row.
Cast off in rib.

MAKING UP

Press all pieces with a warm iron over a damp cloth.
Join right shoulder seam using back stitch or mattress stitch if preferred.

Neckband

With RS facing and using 3¾mm (US 5) needles, pick up and knit 40 (42: 42: 44: 46: 48) sts down left side of neck to first marker, 17 sts down rest of left side of neck to next marker, 14 (16: 16: 18: 18: 18) sts from front to next marker, 17 sts up right side of neck to next marker, 40 (42: 42: 44: 46: 48) sts up rest of right side of neck, 12 sts down right side of back neck, 38 (40: 40: 42: 42: 42) sts from back, and 12 sts up left side of back neck.
190 (198: 198: 206: 210: 214) sts.
Work in g st for 3 rows, ending with a WS row.
Change to 3¼mm (US 3) needles.
Work in g st for a further 4 rows, ending with a WS row.

Row 8 (RS): K40 (42: 42: 44: 46: 48), *(K2tog, K3) 3 times, K2tog*, K14 (16: 16: 18: 18: 18), rep from * to * once more, K40 (42: 42: 44: 46: 48), **(K2tog, K3) twice, K2tog**, K38 (40: 40: 42: 42: 42), rep from ** to ** once more.
176 (184: 184: 192: 196: 200) sts.
Work in g st for 3 rows, ending with a WS row.

Row 12 (RS): K1, *K2tog, yfwd, rep from * to last st, K1.

Row 13: Knit.

Row 14: K39 (41: 41: 43: 45: 47), *(K2tog, K2) 3 times, K2tog*, K14 (16: 16: 18: 18: 18), rep from * to * once more, K39 (41: 41: 43: 45: 47), **(K2tog, K2) twice, K2tog**, K36 (38: 38: 40: 40: 40), rep from ** to ** once more.
Cast off rem 162 (170: 170: 178: 182: 186) sts knitwise (on WS).

Join left shoulder and neckband seam. Join side seams. Join sleeve seams. Sew sleeves into armholes.

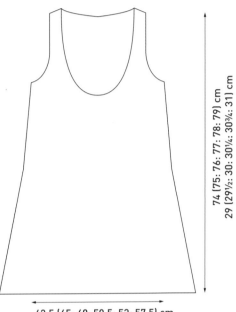

42.5 (45: 48: 50.5: 53: 57.5) cm
16¾ (17¾: 19: 20: 21: 22½) in

74 (75: 76: 77: 78: 79) cm
29 (29½: 30: 30¼: 30¾: 31) cm

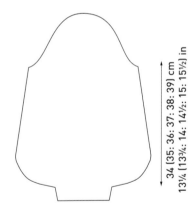

34 (35: 36: 37: 38: 39) cm
13¼ (13¾: 14: 14½: 15: 15½) in

SMOULDER

Boxy sweater worked in an open fabric

Recommendation

Suitable for the novice knitter
Please see pages 8 & 9 for photographs.

	XS	S	M	L	XL	XXL	
To fit	81	86	91	97	102	109	cm
bust	32	34	36	38	40	43	in

Rowan KidSilk Haze

      4   5   5   6   6   7 x 25gm

Photographed in Anthracite

Needles

1 pair 4mm (no 8) (US 6) needles
1 pair 4½mm (no 7) (US 7) needles
1 pair 8mm (no 0) (US 11) needles
1 pair 9mm (no 00) (US 13) needles
4.00mm (no 8) (US G6) crochet hook

Tension

12 sts and 19 rows to 10 cm measured over
pattern using a combination of 4½mm (US 7)
and 9mm (US 13) needles and yarn DOUBLE.

BACK

Cast on 51 (55: 57: 61: 63: 69) sts using
8mm (US 11) needles and yarn DOUBLE.
**Row 1 (RS): Using 4mm (US 6) needle,
knit.
Row 2: Using 8mm (US 11) needle, purl.
Rows 3 to 8: As rows 1 and 2, 3 times.
Change needles and now work in patt as folls:
Row 9 (RS): Using 4½mm (US 7) needle,
knit.
Row 10: Using 9mm (US 13) needle, purl.
Rows 9 and 10 form patt.**
Cont in patt until back measures 34 (34: 35:
35: 35: 35) cm, ending with a WS row.
Shape armholes
Keeping patt correct, cast off 3 sts at beg
of next 2 rows.
45 (49: 51: 55: 57: 63) sts.
Dec 1 st at each end of next 3 (3: 3: 5: 5: 5)
rows, then on foll 1 (1: 1: 1: 1: 3) alt rows,
then on 0 (1: 1: 1: 1: 1) foll 4th row.
37 (39: 41: 41: 43: 45) sts.
Cont straight until armhole measures 18 (19:
19: 20: 21: 22) cm, ending with a WS row.
Shape back neck and shoulders
Next row (RS): Cast off 3 (3: 3: 3: 3: 4) sts,
K until there are 7 (7: 8: 7: 8: 8) sts on right
needle and turn, leaving rem sts on a holder.
Work each side of neck separately.
Cast off 4 sts at beg of next row.
Cast off rem 3 (3: 4: 3: 4: 4) sts.
With RS facing, rejoin yarn to rem sts, cast off
centre 17 (19: 19: 21: 21: 21) sts, K to end.
Complete to match first side, reversing
shapings.

FRONT

Work as given for back until 12 (12: 12: 14:
14: 14) rows less have been worked than on
back to start of shoulder shaping, ending with
a WS row.
Shape front neck
Next row (RS): K12 (12: 13: 13: 14: 15)
and turn, leaving rem sts on a holder.
Work each side of neck separately.
Keeping patt correct, dec 1 st at neck edge
of next 4 rows, then on foll 2 (2: 2: 3: 3: 3)
alt rows.
6 (6: 7: 6: 7: 8) sts.
Work 3 rows, ending with a WS row.

Shape shoulder

Cast off 3 (3: 3: 3: 3: 4) sts at beg of next row.
Work 1 row.
Cast off rem 3 (3: 4: 3: 4: 4) sts.
With RS facing, rejoin yarn to rem sts, cast off
centre 13 (15: 15: 15: 15: 15) sts, K to end.
Complete to match first side, reversing shapings.

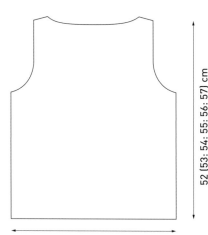

52 [53: 54: 55: 56: 57] cm
20½ [21: 21¼: 21¾: 22: 22½] in

43 (46: 47.5: 51: 52.5: 57.5) cm
17 (18: 18¾: 20: 20¾: 22½) in

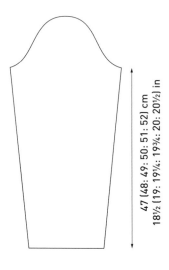

47 (48: 49: 50: 51: 52) cm
18½ (19: 19¼: 19¾: 20: 20½) in

Continued on next page...

Recommendation

Suitable for the knitter with a little experience
Please see pages 26, 27 & 37 for photographs.

	XS	S	M	L	XL	XXL	
To fit	**81**	**86**	**91**	**97**	**102**	**109**	cm
bust	32	34	36	38	40	43	in

Rowan All Seasons Cotton

| | 9 | 10 | 11 | 12 | 13 | 15 | x 50gm |

Photographed in Bleached

Needles

1 pair 4½mm (no 7) (US 7) needles

Tension

21 sts and 30 rows to 10 cm measured over
pattern using 4½mm (US 7) needles.

CAMEO
Ribbed jacket with deep raglans

BACK

Cast on 87 (93: 99: 103: 109: 117) sts using
4½mm (US 7) needles.
Row 1 (RS): K3 (2: 1: 3: 2: 2), P1, *K3, P1, rep
from * to last 3 (2: 1: 3: 2: 2) sts, K3 (2: 1: 3: 2: 2).
Row 2: K1 (0: 3: 1: 0: 0), P1, *K3, P1, rep from
* to last 1 (0: 3: 1: 0: 0) sts, K1 (0: 3: 1: 0: 0).
These 2 rows form patt.
Cont in patt until back measures 18 (18: 19:
19: 19: 19) cm, ending with a WS row.

Shape raglan armholes

Keeping patt correct, cast off 6 (5: 4: 6: 5: 5) sts at
beg of next 2 rows.
75 (83: 91: 91: 99: 107) sts.
Work 2 rows, ending with a WS row.
Next row (RS): K1, P1, K3, P2tog, patt to last
7 sts, P2tog tbl, K3, P1, K1.
Next row: K3, P1, K2, patt to last 6 sts, K2, P1, K3.
Next row: K1, P1, K3, P1, patt to last 6 sts, P1,
K3, P1, K1.
Next row: K3, P1, K2, patt to last 6 sts, K2, P1, K3.
Rep last 4 rows 8 (6: 2: 5: 2: 0) times
more.
57 (69: 85: 79: 93: 105) sts.
Next row (RS): K1, P1, K3, P2tog, patt to last
7 sts, P2tog tbl, K3, P1, K1.

Next row: K3, P1, K2, patt to last 6 sts, K2, P1, K3.
Rep last 2 rows 15 (20: 28: 24: 31: 37) times,
ending with a WS row.
Cast off rem 25 (27: 27: 29: 29: 29) sts.

LEFT FRONT

Cast on 37 (40: 43: 45: 48: 52) sts using
4½mm (US 7) needles.
Row 1 (RS): K3 (2: 1: 3: 2: 2), P1, *K3, P1, rep
from * to last 5 sts, K5.
Row 2: *K3, P1, rep from * to last 1 (0: 3: 1: 0:
0) sts, K1 (0: 3: 1: 0: 0).
These 2 rows form patt.
Cont in patt until left front matches back to start
of raglan armhole shaping, ending with a WS row.

Shape raglan armhole

Keeping patt correct, cast off 6 (5: 4: 6: 5: 5)
sts at beg of next row.
31 (35: 39: 39: 43: 47) sts.
Work 3 rows, ending with a WS row.
Working all decreases as set by back raglan, dec
1 st at raglan armhole edge of next and 9 (7: 3: 6:
3: 1) foll 4th rows, then on foll 7 (12: 20: 16: 23:
29) alt rows.
14 (15: 15: 16: 16: 16) sts.
Work 1 row, ending with a WS row.

Continued on next page...

SMOULDER – Continued from previous page.

SLEEVES (both alike)

Cast on 22 (24: 26: 26: 28: 28) sts using 8mm
(US 11) needles and yarn DOUBLE.
Work as given for back from ** to **.
Work in patt for 6 rows, ending with a WS row.
Row 17 (RS): K3, M1, K to last 3 sts, M1, K3.
24 (26: 28: 28: 30: 30) sts.
Working all increases as set by last row, cont
in patt, shaping sides by inc 1 st at each end
of 10th (10th: 10th: 10th: 12th: 12th) and
every foll 10th (10th: 10th: 12th: 12th: 12th)
row to 32 (32: 32: 40: 42: 40) sts, then on
every foll 12th (12th: 12th: -: -: 14th) row until
there are 36 (38: 40: -: -: 42) sts.

Cont straight until sleeve measures 47 (48: 49:
50: 51: 52) cm, ending with a WS row.

Shape top

Keeping patt correct, cast off 3 sts at beg
of next 2 rows.
30 (32: 34: 34: 36: 36) sts.
Dec 1 st at each end of next and foll alt row,
then on 3 (4: 3: 3: 3: 3) foll 4th rows.
20 (20: 24: 24: 26: 26) sts.
Work 1 row, ending with a WS row.
Dec 1 st at each end of next and foll 2 (0: 2:
2: 3: 3) alt rows, then on foll 1 (3: 3: 3: 3: 3)
rows, ending with a WS row.
Cast off rem 12 sts.

MAKING UP

Press all pieces with a warm iron over
a damp cloth.
Join both shoulder seams using back stitch
or mattress stitch if preferred.

Neck edging

With RS facing, 4.00mm (US G6) crochet
hook and yarn DOUBLE, attach yarn to
neck edge at left shoulder point and work
one round of double crochet evenly around
entire neck edge.
Fasten off.
Join side seams. Join sleeve seams.
Sew sleeves into armholes.

Place marker after 6th st in from end of last row.

Next row (RS): Patt to within 2 sts of marker, P2tog, patt to end.

Work 1 row.

Rep last 2 rows 4 times more.

9 (10: 10: 11: 11: 11) sts.

Next row (RS): Work 2 tog, patt to end.

Cont in patt on these 8 (9: 9: 10: 10: 10) sts only for a further 33 (35: 35: 37: 37: 37) rows (for back neck border extension), ending with a WS row.

Cast off.

RIGHT FRONT

Cast on 37 (40: 43: 45: 48: 52) sts using 4½mm (US 7) needles.

Row 1 (RS): K5, P1, *K3, P1, rep from * to last 3 (2: 1: 3: 2: 2) sts, K3 (2: 1: 3: 2: 2).

Row 2: K1 (0: 3: 1: 0: 0), *P1, K3, rep from * to end.

These 2 rows form patt.

Complete to match left front, reversing all shapings.

SLEEVES (both alike)

Cast on 95 (97: 99: 103: 105: 109) sts using 4½mm (US 7) needles.

Beg with patt row 1, work in patt as given for back until sleeve measures 18 (18: 19: 19: 19: 19) cm, ending with a WS row.

Shape raglan

Keeping patt correct, cast off 6 (5: 4: 6: 5: 5) sts at beg of next 2 rows.

83 (87: 91: 91: 95: 99) sts.

Work 2 (0: 0: 0: 0: 0) rows, ending with a WS row.

Sizes M, XL and XXL only

Next row (RS): K1, P1, K3, P2tog, patt to last 7 sts, P2tog tbl, K3, P1, K1.

Next row: K3, P1, K1, K2tog tbl, patt to last 7 sts, K2tog, K1, P1, K3.

Rep last 2 rows - (-: 1: -: 0: 0) times more.

- (-: 83: -: 91: 95) sts.

All sizes

Next row (RS): K1, P1, K3, P2tog, patt to last 7 sts, P2tog tbl, K3, P1, K1.

Next row: K3, P1, K2, patt to last 6 sts, K2, P1, K3.

Rep last 2 rows 31 (33: 31: 35: 35: 37) times, ending with a WS row. 19 sts.

Keeping raglan decreases correct as set, cont as folls:

Left sleeve only

Dec 1 st at each end of next row, then cast off 5 sts at beg of foll row. 12 sts.

Dec 1 st at beg of next row, then cast off 6 sts at beg of foll row.

Right sleeve only

Cast off 6 sts at beg and dec 1 st at end of next row. 12 sts. Work 1 row.

Cast off 7 sts at beg of next row.

Work 1 row.

Both sleeves

Cast off rem 5 sts.

MAKING UP

Press all pieces with a warm iron over a damp cloth.

Join all raglan seams using back stitch or mattress stitch if preferred.

Join cast-off ends of back neck border extensions, then sew one edge to top of sleeves and back neck. Join side and sleeve seams.

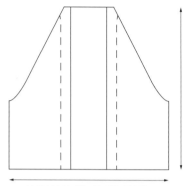

42 (43: 44: 45: 46: 47) cm
16½ (17: 17¼: 17¾: 18: 18½) in

41.5 (44.5: 47: 49: 52: 55.5) cm
16¼ (17¼: 18½: 19¼: 20½: 21¾) in

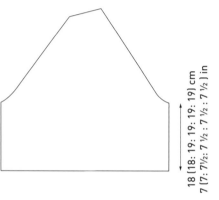

18 (18: 19: 19: 19: 19) cm
7 (7: 7½: 7½: 7½: 7½) in

Recommendation

Suitable for the crocheter with a little experience
Please see pages 14, 15 & 16 for photographs.

	XS	S	M	L	XL	XXL
To fit	81	86	91	97	102	109
cm						
bust	32	34	36	38	40	43
in						

Rowan Handknit Cotton

| | 12 | 13 | 14 | 15 | 16 | 17 | x 50gm |

Photographed in Bleached

Crochet hook

4.00mm (no 8) (US G6) crochet hook
3.50mm (no 9) (US E4) crochet hook

Buttons – 5 button frames

Tension

16 sts and 14 rows to 10 cm measured over
pattern using 4.00mm (US G6) crochet hook.

Crochet abbreviations

ch = chain; **dc** = double crochet; **dc2tog** =
(insert hook as indicated, yoh and draw loop
through) twice, yoh and draw through all 3
loops; **ss** = slip stitch; **tr** = treble; **tr2tog** =
(yoh and insert hook as indicated, yoh and
draw loop through, yoh and draw through 2
loop) twice, yoh and draw through all 3 loop;
yoh = yarn over hook.

SALICE
Fitted crochet cardigan

BACK

Make 64 (68: 72: 76: 80: 86) ch using
4.00mm (US G6) hook.
Foundation row (RS): 1 tr into 5th ch from hook,
1 tr into ch **before** one just worked into enclosing
previous tr in this st, *miss next ch, 1 tr into next
ch, 1 tr into missed ch enclosing previous tr in this
st, rep from * to last ch, 1 tr into last ch, turn.
62 (66: 70: 74: 78: 84) sts.
Now work in patt as folls:
Row 1 (WS): 1 ch (does NOT count as st), 1
dc into each tr to end, working last dc into top
of 3 ch at beg of previous row, turn.
Row 2: 3 ch (counts as first tr), miss dc at
base of 3 ch, *miss next dc, 1 tr into next dc,
1 tr into missed dc enclosing previous tr in this
st, rep from * to last dc, 1 tr into last dc, turn.
These 2 rows form patt.
Cont in patt for a further 7 rows.
Row 10 (RS): 3 ch (counts as first tr), miss
dc at base of 3 ch, tr2tog over next 2 dc -
1 st decreased, patt to last 3 dc, tr2tog over
next 2 dc - 1 st decreased, 1 tr into last dc, turn.
60 (64: 68: 72: 76: 82) sts.
Row 11: 1 ch (does NOT count as st), 1 dc into
each st to end, working last dc into top
of 3 ch at beg of previous row, turn.
Row 12: 3 ch (counts as first tr), miss dc at
base of 3 ch, 1 tr into next dc, patt to last 2 dc,
1 tr into each of last 2 dc, turn.
Work 1 row.
Row 14: 3 ch (does NOT count as st), miss dc
at base of 3 ch - 1 st decreased, 1 tr into next
dc, patt to last 2 dc, tr2tog over last 2 dc - 1 st
decreased, turn.
58 (62: 66: 70: 74: 80) sts.
Work 9 rows.
Row 24 (RS): 3 ch (counts as first tr), 1 tr
into dc at base of 3 ch - 1 st increased, patt
to last dc, 2 tr into last dc - 1 st increased, turn.
60 (64: 68: 72: 76: 82) sts.
Work 1 row.
Row 26: 3 ch (counts as first tr), miss dc at
base of 3 ch, 1 tr into next dc, patt to last 2 dc,
1 tr into each of last 2 dc, turn.
Work 1 row.
Row 28 (RS): 3 ch (counts as first tr), miss dc
at base of 3 ch, 1 tr into next dc, 1 tr into dc at
base of 3 ch enclosing previous tr in this st - 1
st increased, patt to last 2 dc, miss 1 dc, 1 tr

into last dc, 1 tr into dc just missed enclosing
previous tr in this st, 1 tr into last dc - 1 st
increased, turn. 62 (66: 70: 74: 78: 84) sts.
Work 3 rows.
Rep last 8 rows once more.
66 (70: 74: 78: 82: 88) sts.
Working all sts in patt as now set, cont
straight until back measures approx
32 (32: 33: 33: 33: 33) cm, ending with
a WS row.
Shape armholes
Next row (RS): Ss across and into 4th dc,
3 ch (counts as first tr), miss dc at base
of 3 ch, 1 tr into next dc - 3 sts decreased,
patt to last 5 dc, 1 tr into each of next 2
dc and turn, leaving rem 3 sts unworked
- 3 sts decreased. 60 (64: 68: 72: 76: 82) sts.
Next row: 1 ch (does NOT count as st), dc2tog
over first 2 tr - 1 st decreased, 1 dc into each
st to last 2 sts, dc2tog over last 2 sts - 1 st
decreased, turn. 58 (62: 66: 70: 74: 80) sts.
Next row: 3 ch (counts as first tr), miss dc
at base of 3 ch, tr2tog over next 2 dc - 1 st
decreased, patt to last 3 dc, tr2tog over next
2 dc - 1 st decreased, 1 tr into last dc, turn.
56 (60: 64: 68: 72: 78) sts.
Next row: 1 ch (does NOT count as st), dc2tog
over first 2 tr - 1 st decreased, 1 dc into each
st to last 2 sts, dc2tog over last 2 sts - 1 st
decreased, turn. 54 (58: 62: 66: 70: 76) sts.
Rep last 2 rows 1 (1: 2: 2: 3: 4) times more.
50 (54: 54: 58: 58: 60) sts.
Cont straight until armhole measures approx
16 (17: 17: 18: 19: 20) cm, ending with
a **RS** row.
Shape back neck
Next row (WS): Patt first 14 (15: 15:
16: 16: 17) sts and turn, leaving rem
sts unworked.
Next row: 3 ch (does NOT count as st),
miss dc at base of 3 ch, 1 tr into each of
next 0 (1: 1: 0: 0: 1) dc, patt to end, turn.
Work 1 row on these 13 (14: 14: 15: 15: 16) sts.
Fasten off.
Return to last complete row worked, miss next
22 (24: 24: 26: 26: 26) sts, attach yarn to next
st and cont as folls:
Next row (WS): 1 ch (does NOT count as st),
1 dc into st at base of 1 ch, 1 dc into each st to
end, turn. 14 (15: 15: 16: 16: 17) sts.

Next row: 3 ch (counts as first tr), miss dc at base of 3 ch, patt next 10 (12: 12: 12: 12: 14) sts, (1 tr into next dc) 1 (0: 0: 1: 1: 0) times, tr2tog over next 2 dc and turn, leaving rem sts unworked.

Work 1 row on these 13 (14: 14: 15: 15: 16) sts. Fasten off.

POCKET LININGS (make 2)

Make 20 (20: 20: 22: 22: 22) ch using 4.00mm (US G6) hook.

Work foundation row as given for back. 18 (18: 18: 20: 20: 20) sts.

Beg with row 1, work in patt as given for back for 12 rows, ending with a **RS** row. Break yarn.

LEFT FRONT

Make 38 (40: 42: 44: 46: 48) ch using 4.00mm (US G6) hook.

Work foundation row as given for back. 36 (38: 40: 42: 44: 46) sts.

Now work in patt as given for back for 9 rows, ending with a WS row.

Working all decreases and increases as given for back, cont as folls:

Dec 1 st at beg of next and foll 4th row, ending with a **RS** row. 34 (36: 38: 40: 42: 44) sts.

Place pocket

Next row (WS): Patt 12 (12: 12: 14: 14: 14) sts, miss next 18 (18: 18: 20: 20: 20) sts and, in their place, patt across 18 (18: 18: 20: 20: 20) sts of first pocket lining, patt rem 4 (6: 8: 6: 8: 10) sts, turn.

Work 8 rows.

Inc 1 st at beg of next and 3 foll 4th rows. 38 (40: 42: 44: 46: 48) sts.

Cont straight until left front matches back to beg of armhole shaping, ending with a WS row.

Shape armhole

Dec 3 sts at beg of next row. 35 (37: 39: 41: 43: 45) sts.

Dec 1 st at armhole edge of next 5 (5: 7: 7: 9: 11) rows. 30 (32: 32: 34: 34: 34) sts.

Cont straight until 11 rows less have been worked than on back to shoulder fasten-off, ending with a **RS** row. Break yarn.

Shape neck

Next row (WS): Miss first 12 (13: 13: 14: 14: 13) sts, attach yarn to next st, 1 ch (does **NOT** count as st), 1 dc into st at base of 1 ch, patt to end, turn. 18 (19: 19: 20: 20: 21) sts.

Dec 1 st at neck edge of next 5 rows. 13 (14: 14: 15: 15: 16) sts.

Work a further 5 rows, ending with a WS row. Fasten off.

RIGHT FRONT

Make 38 (40: 42: 44: 46: 48) ch using 4.00mm (US G6) hook.

Work foundation row as given for back. 36 (38: 40: 42: 44: 46) sts.

Now work in patt as given for back for 9 rows, ending with a WS row.

Working all decreases and increases as given for back, cont as folls:

Dec 1 st at end of next and foll 4th row, ending with a **RS** row. 34 (36: 38: 40: 42: 44) sts.

Place pocket

Next row (WS): Patt 4 (6: 8: 6: 8: 10) sts, miss next 18 (18: 18: 20: 20: 20) sts and, in their place, patt across 18 (18: 18: 20: 20: 20) sts of second pocket lining, patt rem 12 (12: 12: 14: 14: 14) sts, turn.

Complete to match left front, reversing shapings and working first row of neck shaping as folls:

Shape neck

Next row (WS): Patt to last 12 (13: 13: 14: 14: 13) sts and turn, leaving rem sts unworked. 18 (19: 19: 20: 20: 21) sts.

SLEEVES (both alike)

First cuff section

Make 22 (22: 24: 24: 24: 26) ch using 4.00mm (US G6) hook.

Work foundation row as given for back. 20 (20: 22: 22: 22: 24) sts.

Now work in patt as given for back for 8 rows, ending with a **RS** row. Break yarn.

Second cuff section

Work as given for first cuff section but do **NOT** break yarn.

Join sections

Next row (WS): 1 ch (does **NOT** count as st), 1 dc into each st of second cuff section, then 1 dc into each st of first cuff section, turn. 40 (40: 44: 44: 44: 48) sts.

Working all increases as given for back, cont as folls:

Inc 1 st at each end of 3rd and every foll 8th (6th: 12th: 10th: 8th: 10th) row until there are 48 (50: 50: 52: 54: 56) sts, taking inc sts into patt.

Cont straight until sleeve measures approx 32 (33: 34: 35: 36: 37) cm, ending with a WS row.

Shape top

Working all decreases as set by back armhole, dec 3 sts at each end of next row. 42 (44: 44: 46: 48: 50) sts.

Dec 1 st at each end of next 4 rows, then on every foll alt row to 28 sts, then on foll 7 rows, ending with a WS row. 14 sts. Fasten off.

MAKING UP

Press all pieces with a warm iron over a damp cloth.

Join both shoulder seams using back stitch or mattress stitch if preferred. Mark points along side seam edges of back and fronts 6 cm up from foundation ch edge.

Lower back edging

With RS facing and using 4.00mm (US G6) crochet hook, attach yarn to left side seam edge of back at marker, 1 ch (does **NOT** count as st), now work 1 row of dc down left back side opening edge, across foundation ch edge, then up right side seam edge to other marker, working 3 dc into each corner point, do **NOT** turn.

Now work 1 row of crab st (dc worked from left to right instead of right to left) along this edge. Fasten off.

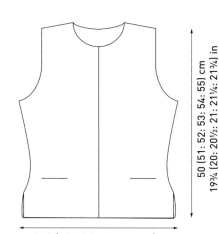

50 (51: 52: 53: 54: 55) cm
19¾ (20: 20½: 21: 21¼: 21¾) in

41.5 (44: 46.5: 49: 51.5: 55) cm
16¼ (17¼: 18¼: 19¼: 20: 21½) in

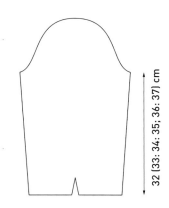

32 (33: 34: 35: 36: 37) cm

Continued on next page...

Recommendation
Suitable for the knitter with a little experience
Please see pages 36 & 42 for photographs.

One size

Rowan Cotton Glace
2 x 50gm
Photographed in Dawn Grey & Black

Needles
1 pair 2¾mm (no 12) (US 2) needles
1 pair 3¼mm (no 10) (US 3) needles

Tension
24 sts and 39 rows to 10 cm measured over
pattern using 3¼mm (US 3) needles.

CAMELLIA
Close fitting hat with pretty detail

HAT
Cast on 111 sts using 2¾mm (US 2) needles.
Rows 1 to 3: Knit.
Row 4 (WS): K1, *P1, K1, rep from * to end.
Row 5: As row 4.
Last 2 rows form moss st.
Work in moss st for a further 5 rows, ending
with a WS row.
Change to 3¼mm (US 3) needles.
Beg with a K row, work in st st for 4 rows,
ending with a WS row.
Row 15 (RS): K1, *yfwd, K2tog, rep from
* to end.
Beg with a K row, work in rev st st for 3 rows,
ending with a WS row.
Beg with a K row, work in st st for 3 rows,
ending with a RS row.
Work in moss st for 5 rows, ending with a WS row.
Beg with a K row, work in st st for 3 rows,
ending with a RS row.
Beg with a K row, work in rev st st for 3 rows,
ending with a WS row.
Beg with a K row, work in st st for 2 rows,
ending with a WS row.
Row 35 (RS): As row 15.
Row 36: P2, *yrn, P2tog, rep from * to last st, P1.
Beg with a K row, work in st st for 3 rows,
ending with a RS row.
Beg with a K row, work in rev st st for 4 rows,
ending with a RS row.

Beg with a P row, work in st st for 2 rows,
ending with a RS row.
Row 46 (WS): Knit.
Row 47: As row 15.
Row 48: Knit.
Beg with a K row, now complete hat in st
st as folls:
Work 1 row, ending with a RS row.
Shape top
Row 1 (WS): P1, (P2tog, P9) 10 times. 101 sts.
Work 3 rows.
Row 5: P1, (P2tog, P8) 10 times. 91 sts.
Work 3 rows.
Row 9: P1, (P2tog, P7) 10 times. 81 sts.
Work 1 row.
Row 11: P1, (P2tog, P6) 10 times. 71 sts.
Work 1 row.
Row 13: P1, (P2tog, P5) 10 times. 61 sts.
Work 1 row.
Row 15: P1, (P2tog, P4) 10 times. 51 sts.
Work 1 row.
Row 17: P1, (P2tog, P3) 10 times. 41 sts.
Work 1 row.
Row 19: P1, (P2tog, P2) 10 times. 31 sts.
Row 20: (K1, K2tog) 10 times, K1.
21 sts.
Row 21: P1, (P2tog) 10 times.
Break yarn and thread through rem 11 sts.
Pull up tight and fasten off securely.
Join back seam.

SALICE – *Continued from previous page.*

Front and neck edging
Starting and ending at markers along front
side seam edges, work edging along front
foundation ch edges, front openings edges
and neck edge in same way as given for lower
back edging.
Pocket edgings (both alike)
Work edging across pocket opening edge in
same way as given for lower back edging.
Neatly sew pocket linings in place on
inside.

Sleeve edgings (both alike)
Join sleeve seams.
Starting and ending at top of sleeve cuff
opening, work edging along row-end edges of
cuff opening and foundation ch edge in same
way as given for lower back edging.
Join side seams above markers. Sew sleeves
into armholes.
Using two strands of yarn, cover button frames
foll instructions on packet. Sew on buttons,
using "holes" of patt as buttonholes.

Recommendation

Suitable for the more experienced knitter
Please see pages 24 & 25 for photographs.

	XS	S	M	L	XL	XXL	
To fit	**81**	**86**	**91**	**97**	**102**	**109**	cm
bust	32	34	36	38	40	43	in

Rowan Handknit Cotton
26 27 28 30 32 34 x 50gm
Photographed in Slate

Needles

1 pair 3¼mm (no 10) (US 3) needles
1 pair 4mm (no 8) (US 6) needles
Cable needle

Shoulder pads (optional)

Buttons – 14 large and 2 small

Tension

21 sts and 30 rows to 10 cm measured over
double moss stitch using 4mm (US 6) needles.

Special abbreviations

C4B = slip next 2 sts onto cn and leave at back
of work, K2, then K2 from cn; **C4F** = slip next 2
sts onto cn and leave at front of work, K2, then
K2 from cn; **C6B** = slip next 3 sts onto cn and
leave at back of work, K3, then K3 from cn;
C6F = slip next 3 sts onto cn and leave at front
of work, K3, then K3 from cn; **C8B** = slip next
4 sts onto cn and leave at back of work, K4,
then K4 from cn; **C8F** = slip next 4 sts onto cn
and leave at front of work, K4, then K4 from cn.

TORA
Classic trench coat with cable & epaulets

BACK

Cast on 123 (129: 135: 139: 145: 153) sts
using 4mm (US 6) needles.
Row 1 (RS): K0 (1: 0: 0: 1: 1), (P1, K1) 10
(11: 13: 14: 15: 17) times, *P1, K1, inc in next
st, K1, P2, (K1, inc in next st, K1) 4 times, P2,
K1, inc in next st, K1, P1*, (K1, P1) 17 times,
K1, rep from * to * once more, (K1, P1) 10 (11:
13: 14: 15: 17) times, K0 (1: 0: 0: 1: 1). 135
(141: 147: 151: 157: 165) sts.
Row 2: K0 (1: 0: 0: 1: 1), (P1, K1) 10 (11:
13: 14: 15: 17) times, *K1, P4, K2, P16, K2,
P4, K1*, (K1, P1) 17 times, K1, rep from * to
* once more, (K1, P1) 10 (11: 13: 14: 15: 17)
times, K0 (1: 0: 0: 1: 1).
Row 3: P0 (1: 0: 0: 1: 1), (K1, P1) 10 (11: 13:
14: 15: 17) times, *P1, C4B, P2, K16, P2, C4F,
P1*, (P1, K1) 17 times, P1, rep from * to * once
more, (P1, K1) 10 (11: 13: 14: 15: 17) times,
P0 (1: 0: 0: 1: 1).
Row 4: P0 (1: 0: 0: 1: 1), (K1, P1) 10 (11: 13:
14: 15: 17) times, *K1, P4, K2, P16, K2, P4,
K1*, (P1, K1) 17 times, P1, rep from * to * once
more, (P1, K1) 10 (11: 13: 14: 15: 17) times,
P0 (1: 0: 0: 1: 1).
These 4 rows form double moss st either side
of cable panels and between cable panels.
Keeping double moss st correct, cont as folls:
Row 5: Patt 20 (23: 26: 28: 31: 35) sts,
P1, K4, P2, K16, P2, K4, P1, patt 35 sts,
rep from * to * once more, patt 20 (23:
26: 28: 31: 35) sts.
Row 6: Patt 20 (23: 26: 28: 31: 35) sts,
K1, P4, K2, P16, K2, P4, K1, patt 35 sts,
rep from * to * once more, patt 20 (23:
26: 28: 31: 35) sts.
Rows 7 and 8: As rows 5 and 6.
Row 9: Patt 20 (23: 26: 28: 31: 35) sts, *P1,
C4F, P2, K16, P2, C4B, P1*, patt 35 sts, rep
from * to * once more, patt 20 (23: 26: 28: 31:
35) sts.
Row 10: As row 6.
Rows 11 and 12: As rows 5 and 6.
Row 13: Patt 20 (23: 26: 28: 31: 35) sts,
*place marker on right needle, P1, K4, P2, K16,
P2, K4, P1, place marker on right needle*, patt
35 sts, rep from * to * once more, patt 20 (23:
26: 28: 31: 35) sts.
Rows 2 to 13 form cable patt for side cables of
cable panel.

Keeping patt correct as now set and slipping
markers from left needle to right needle on
every row, cont as folls:
Work 7 rows, ending with a WS row.
Row 21: Patt to marker, *patt 7 sts, C8F, C8B,
patt 7 sts*, patt to next marker, rep from * to *
once more, patt to end.
Work 19 rows, dec 1 st at each end of 6th
row and ending with a WS row.
133 (139: 145: 149: 155: 163) sts.
Row 41: Work 2 tog, patt to marker, *patt 7
sts, C8F, C8B, patt 7 sts*, patt to next marker,
rep from * to * once more, patt to last 2 sts,
work 2 tog.
131 (137: 143: 147: 153: 161) sts.
Work 19 rows, dec 1 st at each end of 14th row
and ending with a WS row.
129 (135: 141: 145: 151: 159) sts.
Row 61: Patt to marker, *patt 7 sts, C8F, C8B,
patt 7 sts*, patt to next marker, rep from * to *
once more, patt to end.
Work 11 rows, dec 1 st at each end of 8th row
and ending with a WS row.
127 (133: 139: 143: 149: 157) sts.
Row 73: Patt to marker, *patt 5 sts, P2tog
tbl, K16, P2tog, patt 5 sts*, patt to next
marker, rep from * to * once more,
patt to end.
123 (129: 135: 139: 145: 153) sts.
Now working one st either side of large cable
(instead of 2), cont as folls:
Work 5 rows.
Row 79: Patt to marker, *patt 6 sts, C8F, C8B,
patt 6 sts*, patt to next marker, rep from * to *
once more, patt to end.
Work 15 rows, dec 1 st at each end of 4th row
and ending with a WS row.
121 (127: 133: 137: 143: 151) sts.
Row 95: As row 79.
Work 15 rows, dec 1 st at each end of 2nd row
and ending with a WS row.
119 (125: 131: 135: 141: 149) sts.
Row 111: Work 2 tog, patt to marker, *patt 6
sts, C8F, C8B, patt 6 sts*, patt to next marker,
rep from * to * once more, patt to last 2 sts,
work 2 tog. 117 (123: 129: 133: 139: 147) sts.
Work 13 rows, ending with a WS row.
Row 125: Work 2 tog, patt to marker, *patt 6
sts, slip next 4 sts onto cn and leave at front
of work, K2, K2tog, then K2tog, K2 from cn,

slip next 4 sts onto cn and leave at back of work, K2, K2tog, then K2tog, K2 from cn, patt 6 sts*, patt to next marker, rep from * to * once more, patt to last 2 sts, work 2 tog.
107 (113: 119: 123: 129: 137) sts.
Now work in patt for rest of back as folls:
Row 1 (WS): Patt to marker, *patt 6 sts, P12, patt 6 sts*, patt to next marker, rep from * to * once more, patt to end.
Row 2: Patt to marker, *patt 6 sts, K12, patt 6 sts*, patt to next marker, rep from * to * once more, patt to end.
Rows 3 to 8: As rows 1 and 2, 3 times.
Row 9: As row 1.
Row 10: Patt to marker, *patt 6 sts, C6B, C6F, patt 6 sts*, patt to next marker, rep from * to * once more, patt to end.
Rows 11 to 18: As rows 1 and 2, 4 times.
Row 19 and 20: As rows 9 and 10.
Rows 21 to 28: As rows 1 and 2, 4 times.
Row 29: As row 1.
Row 30: Patt to marker, *patt 6 sts, C6F, C6B, patt 6 sts*, patt to next marker, rep from * to * once more, patt to end.
Rows 31 to 38: As rows 1 and 2, 4 times, inc 1 st at each end of 2nd of these rows.
109 (115: 121: 125: 131: 139) sts.
Rows 39 and 40: As rows 29 and 30.
These 40 rows form patt for rest of back.
Keeping patt correct, inc 1 st at each end of 6th and foll 14th row, taking inc sts into double moss st. 113 (119: 125: 129: 135: 143) sts.
Cont straight until back measures 66 (66: 67: 67: 67: 67) cm, ending with a WS row.
Shape armholes
Keeping patt correct, cast off 3 (4: 4: 5: 5: 6) sts at beg of next 2 rows.
107 (111: 117: 119: 125: 131) sts.
Dec 1 st at each end of next 7 (7: 9: 9: 11: 11) rows, then on foll 3 (4: 4: 4: 4: 5) alt rows, then on foll 4th row. 85 (87: 89: 91: 93: 97) sts.
Cont straight until armhole measures 19 (20: 20: 21: 22: 23) cm, ending with a WS row.
Shape shoulders and back neck
Cast off 10 (10: 10: 10: 11: 11) sts at beg of next 2 rows. 65 (67: 69: 71: 71: 75) sts.
Next row (RS): Cast off 10 (10: 10: 10: 11: 11) sts, patt until there are 14 (14: 15: 15: 14: 16) sts on right needle and turn, leaving rem sts on a holder.
Work each side of neck separately.
Cast off 4 sts at beg of next row.
Cast off rem 10 (10: 11: 11: 10: 12) sts.
With RS facing, rejoin yarn to rem sts, cast off centre 17 (19: 19: 21: 21: 21) sts, patt to end.
Complete to match first side, reversing shapings.

POCKET LININGS (make 2)
Cast on 21 sts using 4mm (US 6) needles.
Row 1 (RS): P1, *K1, P1, rep from * to end.
Row 2: As row 1.
Rows 3 and 4: K1, *P1, K1, rep from * to end.
Rep last 4 rows 5 times more, ending with a WS row.
Break yarn and leave sts on a holder.

LEFT FRONT
Cast on 87 (90: 93: 95: 98: 102) sts using 4mm (US 6) needles.
Row 1 (RS): K0 (1: 0: 0: 1: 1), (P1, K1) 10 (11: 13: 14: 15: 17) times, P1, K1, inc in next st, K1, P2, (K1, inc in next st, K1) 4 times, P2, K1, inc in next st, K1, P1, (K1, P1) 19 times, K5.
93 (96: 99: 101: 104: 108) sts.
Row 2: K5, (P1, K1) 19 times, K1, P4, K2, P16, K2, P4, K1, (K1, P1) 10 (11: 13: 14: 15: 17) times, K0 (1: 0: 0: 1: 1).
Row 3: P0 (1: 0: 0: 1: 1), (K1, P1) 10 (11: 13: 14: 15: 17) times, P1, C4B, P2, K16, P2, C4F, P1, (P1, K1) 19 times, K5.
Row 4: K5, (K1, P1) 19 times, K1, P4, K2, P16, K2, P4, K1, (P1, K1) 10 (11: 13: 14: 15: 17) times, P0 (1: 0: 0: 1: 1).
These 4 rows form double moss st either side of cable panel and g st up front opening edge.
Keeping double moss st and g st correct, cont as folls:
Row 5: Patt 20 (23: 26: 28: 31: 35) sts, P1, K4, P2, K16, P2, K4, P1, patt 43 sts.
Row 6: Patt 43 sts, K1, P4, K2, P16, K2, P4, K1, patt 20 (23: 26: 28: 31: 35).
Rows 7 and 8: As rows 5 and 6.
Row 9: Patt 20 (23: 26: 28: 31: 35) sts, P1, C4F, P2, K16, P2, C4B, P1, patt 43 sts.
Row 10: As row 6.
Rows 11 and 12: As rows 5 and 6.
Row 13: Patt 20 (23: 26: 28: 31: 35) sts, place marker on right needle, P1, K4, P2, K16, P2, K4, P1, place marker on right needle, patt 43 sts.
Rows 2 to 13 form cable patt for side cables of cable panel.
Keeping patt correct as now set and slipping markers from left needle to right needle on every row, cont as folls:
Work 7 rows, ending with a WS row.
Row 21: Patt to marker, patt 7 sts, C8F, C8B, patt 7 sts, patt to end.
Work 19 rows, dec 1 st at beg of 6th row and ending with a WS row. 92 (95: 98: 100: 103: 107) sts.
Row 41: Work 2 tog, patt to marker, patt 7 sts, C8F, C8B, patt to end.
91 (94: 97: 99: 102: 106) sts.

Work 19 rows, dec 1 st at beg of 14th row and ending with a WS row.
90 (93: 96: 98: 101: 105) sts.
Row 61: Patt to marker, patt 7 sts, C8F, C8B, patt 7 sts, patt to end.
Work 11 rows, dec 1 st at beg of 8th row and ending with a WS row.
89 (92: 95: 97: 100: 104) sts.
Row 73: Patt to marker, patt 5 sts, P2tog tbl, K16, P2tog, patt 5 sts, patt to end.
87 (90: 93: 95: 98: 102) sts.
Now working one st either side of large cable (instead of 2), cont as folls:
Work 5 rows.
Row 79: Patt to marker, patt 6 sts, C8F, C8B, patt 6 sts, patt to end.
Work 1 row, ending with a WS row.
Place pocket
Row 81: Patt to within 2 sts of marker, slip rem 73 sts on a holder and, in their place, patt across 21 sts of first pocket lining.
35 (38: 41: 43: 46: 50) sts.
Cont on this set of sts only for pocket lining and side front as folls:
Dec 1 st at beg of 2nd and 3 foll 14th rows.
31 (34: 37: 39: 42: 46) sts.
Work 5 rows, ending with a WS row.
Row 131: Patt 10 (13: 16: 18: 21: 25) sts, cast off rem 21 sts.
Break yarn and leave rem 10 (13: 16: 18: 21: 25) sts on another holder.
Return to sts left on first holder, rejoin yarn with RS facing, cast on and K 5 sts, patt to end.
78 sts.
Work on this set of sts only for pocket front as folls:
Row 82 (WS): Patt to last 5 sts, K5.
Row 83: K5, patt to end.
Last 2 rows set the sts - pocket opening edge 5 sts in g st with all other sts in patt as previously set.
Work 11 rows, ending with a WS row.
Row 95: As row 79.
Work 15 rows, ending with a WS row.
Row 111: As row 79.
Work 13 rows, ending with a WS row.
Row 125: Patt to marker, patt 6 sts, slip next 4 sts onto cn and leave at front of work, K2, K2tog, then K2tog, K2 from cn, slip next 4 sts onto cn and leave at back of work, K2, K2tog, then K2tog, K2 from cn, patt 6 sts, patt to end.
74 sts.
Now work in patt as set by patt for rest of back as folls:
Row 1 (WS): Patt to marker, patt 6 sts, P12, patt 6 sts, patt to end.
Row 2: Patt to marker, patt 6 sts, K12, patt 6 sts, patt to end.

Rows 3 to 6: As rows 1 and 2, twice.

Join sections

Next row (WS): Patt to marker, patt 6 sts, P12, patt 6 sts, patt 2 sts, holding RS of pocket lining and side front against WS of pocket front K tog next st of front section with first st of side section, (K tog next st of front section with next st of side section) 4 times, patt to end.
79 (82: 85: 87: 90: 94) sts.
Now cont in patt across all sts as set by patt for rest of back as folls:

Row 8: As row 2.

Row 9: As row 1.

Row 10: Patt to marker, patt 6 sts, C6B, C6F, patt 6 sts, patt to end.
These 10 rows set position of patt as set for rest of back.
Keeping patt correct as now set, work 21 rows, ending with a WS row.
Inc 1 st at beg of next and 2 foll 14th rows, taking inc sts into double moss st.
82 (85: 88: 90: 93: 97) sts.
Cont straight until left front matches back to start of armhole shaping, ending with a WS row.

Shape armhole

Keeping patt correct, cast off 3 (4: 4: 5: 5: 6) sts at beg of next row.
79 (81: 84: 85: 88: 91) sts.
Work 1 row.
Dec 1 st at armhole edge of next 7 (7: 9: 9: 11: 11) rows, then on foll 3 (4: 4: 4: 4: 5) alt rows, then on foll 4th row. 68 (69: 70: 71: 72: 74) sts.
Cont straight until 25 (25: 25: 27: 27: 27) rows less have been worked than on back to start of shoulder shaping, ending with a **RS** row.

Shape front neck

Keeping patt correct, cast off 23 (24: 24: 24: 24: 24) sts at beg of next row.
45 (45: 46: 47: 48: 50) sts.
Dec 1 st at neck edge of next 9 rows, then on foll 5 (5: 5: 6: 6: 6) alt rows, then on foll 4th row. 30 (30: 31: 31: 32: 34) sts.
Work 1 row, ending with a WS row.

Shape shoulder

Cast off 10 (10: 10: 10: 11: 11) sts at beg of next and foll alt row.
Work 1 row.
Cast off rem 10 (10: 11: 11: 10: 12) sts.
Mark position for 5 pairs of buttons along left front opening edge - first pair to come in row 83, last pair to come 2 cm below neck shaping, and rem 3 pairs evenly spaced between.

RIGHT FRONT

Cast on 87 (90: 93: 95: 98: 102) sts using 4mm (US 6) needles.

Row 1 (RS): K5, P1, (K1, P1) 19 times, K1, inc in next st, K1, P2, (K1, inc in next st, K1) 4 times, P2, K1, inc in next st, K1, (P1, K1) 10 (11: 13: 14: 15: 17) times, P1, K0 (1: 0: 0: 1: 1).
93 (96: 99: 101: 104: 108) sts.

Row 2: K0 (1: 0: 0: 1: 1), (P1, K1) 10 (11: 13: 14: 15: 17) times, K1, P4, K2, P16, K2, P4, K1, (K1, P1) 19 times, K5.

Row 3: K5, (P1, K1) 19 times, P1, C4B, P2, K16, P2, C4F, P1, (P1, K1) 10 (11: 13: 14: 15: 17) times, P0 (1: 0: 0: 1: 1).

Row 4: P0 (1: 0: 0: 1: 1), (K1, P1) 10 (11: 13: 14: 15: 17) times, K1, P4, K2, P16, K2, P4, K1, (P1, K1) 19 times, K5.
These 4 rows form double moss st either side of cable panel and g st up front opening edge.
Keeping double moss st and g st correct, cont as folls:

Row 5: Patt 43 sts, P1, K4, P2, K16, P2, K4, P1, patt 20 (23: 26: 28: 31: 35) sts.

Row 6: Patt 20 (23: 26: 28: 31: 35) sts, K1, P4, K2, P16, K2, P4, K1, patt 43 sts.

Rows 7 and 8: As rows 5 and 6.

Row 9: Patt 43 sts, P1, C4F, P2, K16, P2, C4B, P1, patt 20 (23: 26: 28: 31: 35) sts.

Row 10: As row 6.

Rows 11 and 12: As rows 5 and 6.

Row 13: Patt 43 sts, place marker on right needle, P1, K4, P2, K16, P2, K4, P1, place marker on right needle, patt 20 (23: 26: 28: 31: 35) sts.
Rows 2 to 13 form cable patt for side cables of cable panel.
Keeping patt correct as now set and slipping markers from left needle to right needle on every row, cont as folls:
Work 7 rows, ending with a WS row.

Row 21: Patt to marker, patt 7 sts, C8F, C8B, patt 7 sts, patt to end.
Work 19 rows, dec 1 st at end of 6th row and ending with a WS row.
92 (95: 98: 100: 103: 107) sts.

Row 41: Patt to marker, patt 7 sts, C8F, C8B, patt 7 sts, patt to last 2 sts, work 2 tog.
91 (94: 97: 99: 102: 106) sts.
Work 19 rows, dec 1 st at end of 14th row and ending with a WS row.
90 (93: 96: 98: 101: 105) sts.

Row 61: Patt to marker, patt 7 sts, C8F, C8B, patt 7 sts, patt to end.
Work 11 rows, dec 1 st at end of 8th row and ending with a WS row.
89 (92: 95: 97: 100: 104) sts.

Row 73: Patt to marker, patt 5 sts, P2tog tbl, K16, P2tog, patt 5 sts, patt to end.
87 (90: 93: 95: 98: 102) sts.

Now working one st either side of large cable (instead of 2), cont as folls:
Work 5 rows.

Row 79: Patt to marker, patt 6 sts, C8F, C8B, patt 6 sts, patt to end.
Work 1 row, ending with a WS row.

Place pocket

Row 81: Patt to 2 sts beyond second marker, cast on 5 sts and turn, leaving rem 14 (17: 20: 22: 25: 29) sts on a holder. 78 sts.
Cont on this set of sts only for pocket front as folls:

Row 82 (WS): K5, patt to end.

Row 83 (buttonhole row) (RS): K5, cast off 2 sts (to make first buttonhole of first pair - cast on 2 sts over these cast-off sts on next row), patt until there are 24 sts on right needle after cast-off, cast off 2 sts (to make 2nd buttonhole of first pair - cast on 2 sts over these cast-off sts on next row), patt to last 5 sts, K5.
Last 2 rows set the sts - pocket opening edge 5 sts in g st with all other sts in patt as previously set.
Making a further 4 pairs of buttonholes as set by last row worked to correspond with positions marked for buttons on left front and noting that no further reference will be made to buttonholes, cont as folls:
Work 11 rows, ending with a WS row.

Row 95: As row 79.
Work 15 rows, ending with a WS row.

Row 111: As row 79.
Work 13 rows, ending with a WS row.

Row 125: Patt to marker, patt 6 sts, slip next 4 sts onto cn and leave at front of work, K2, K2tog, then K2tog, K2 from cn, slip next 4 sts onto cn and leave at back of work, K2, K2tog, then K2tog, K2 from cn, patt 6 sts, patt to end.
74 sts.
Now work in patt as set by patt for rest of back as folls:

Row 1 (WS): Patt to marker, patt 6 sts, P12, patt 6 sts, patt to end.

Row 2: Patt to marker, patt 6 sts, K12, patt 6 sts, patt to end.

Rows 3 to 6: As rows 1 and 2, twice.
Break yarn and leave 74 sts on another holder.
Return to sts left on first holder, rejoin yarn with RS facing, patt across 21 sts of second pocket lining, then patt sts from holder.
35 (38: 41: 43: 46: 50) sts.
Cont on this set of sts only for pocket lining and side front as folls:
Dec 1 st at end of 2nd and 3 foll 14th rows.
31 (34: 37: 39: 42: 46) sts.
Work 5 rows, ending with a WS row.

Row 131: Cast off 21 sts, patt to end.
10 (13: 16: 18: 21: 25) sts.

Join sections

Next row (WS): Patt first 5 (8: 11: 13: 16: 20) sts, holding RS of pocket lining and side front against WS of pocket front K tog next st of side section with first st of front section, (K tog next st of side section with next st of front section) 4 times, patt to marker, patt 6 sts, P12, patt 6 sts, patt to end. 79 (82: 85: 87: 90: 94) sts.
Now cont in patt across all sts as set by patt for rest of back as folls:
Row 8: As row 2.
Row 9: As row 1.
Row 10: Patt to marker, patt 6 sts, C6B, C6F, patt 6 sts, patt to end.
These 10 rows set position of patt as set for rest of back.
Keeping patt correct as now set, work 21 rows, ending with a WS row.
Inc 1 st at end of next and 2 foll 14th rows, taking inc sts into double moss st.
82 (85: 88: 90: 93: 97) sts.
Complete to match left front, reversing shapings.

SLEEVES (both alike)

Cast on 51 (53: 55: 57: 59: 61) sts using 4mm (US 6) needles.
Row 1 (RS): K1, *P1, K1, rep from * to end.
Row 2: As row 1.
Rows 3 and 4: P1, *K1, P1, rep from * to end.
These 4 rows form double moss st.
Cont in double moss st, shaping sides by inc 1 st at each end of 13th (13th: 17th: 17th: 17th: 19th) and every foll 16th (16th: 20th: 20th: 22nd: 22nd) row to 59 (59: 63: 63: 71: 73) sts, then on every foll 18th (18th: 22nd: 22nd: -: -) row until there are 65 (67: 67: 69: -: -) sts, taking inc sts into patt.
Cont straight until sleeve measures 44 (45: 46: 47: 48: 49) cm, ending with a WS row.

Shape top

Keeping patt correct, cast off 3 (4: 4: 5: 5: 6) sts at beg of next 2 rows. 59 (59: 59: 59: 61: 61) sts.
Dec 1 st at each end of next 3 rows, then on foll alt row, then on foll 4th row, then on 2 (2: 2: 3: 3: 3) foll 6th rows. 45 (45: 45: 43: 45: 45) sts.
Work 3 rows, ending with a WS row.
Dec 1 st at each end of next and 1 (1: 1: 0: 0: 1) foll 4th row, then on foll 2 (4: 4: 4: 5: 4) alt rows, then on foll 5 (3: 3: 3: 3: 3) rows, ending with a WS row.
Cast off rem 27 sts.

MAKING UP

Press all pieces with a warm iron over a damp cloth.
Join both shoulder seams using back stitch or mattress stitch if preferred.

Collar

Cast on 97 (101: 101: 107: 107: 107) sts using 3¼mm (US 3) needles.
Beg with row 1, work in double moss st as given for sleeves for 14 rows, ending with a WS row.
Row 15 (RS): Patt 2 sts, work 3 tog, patt to last 5 sts, work 3 tog tbl, patt 2 sts.
93 (97: 97: 103: 103: 103) sts.
Work 13 rows.
Row 29: As row 15. 89 (93: 93: 99: 99: 99) sts.
Work 13 rows, ending with a WS row.
Cast off 10 sts at beg of next 4 (2: 2: 0: 0: 0) rows, then 11 sts at beg of foll 2 (4: 4: 6: 6: 6) rows.
Cast off rem 27 (29: 29: 33: 33: 33) sts.
Positioning row-end edges of collar 24 sts in from front opening edges, sew shaped cast-off edge of collar to neck edge.

Sleeve and shoulder tabs (make 4)

Cast on 9 sts using 3¼mm (US 3) needles.
Work in g st for 80 (80: 82: 82: 84: 86) rows, ending with a WS row.
Cast off.
Join sleeve seams, inserting one end of a sleeve tab into seam, positioning tab 6 cm up from cast-on edge.
Secure free end of tab by attaching a large button through both layers.

Shoulder tab loops (make 2)

Cast on 12 sts using 3¼mm (US 3) needles.
Cast off.
Join side seams. Insert sleeves. Lay shoulder tab loop next to armhole seam as in photograph and sew ends in place. Thread shoulder tabs through this loop and fold in half, positioning fold over armhole seam.
Secure free ends of tab to shoulder seam by attaching a large button through all layers as in photograph.
Sew pocket linings in place on inside, then neatly sew cast-on edge of pocket border in position.
Sew on rem large buttons to correspond with 5 pairs of buttonholes in right front. At top corners of front opening edges, make a button loop and attach small buttons to correspond.

Belt

Cast on 12 sts using 3¼mm (US 3) needles.
Work in g st until belt measures 135 (140: 145: 150: 155: 160) cm, ending with a WS row.
Cast off.
Try on coat and mark waist position.
Make belt loops at side seams at waist position and thread belt through these loops.
Slip stitch shoulder pads into place.

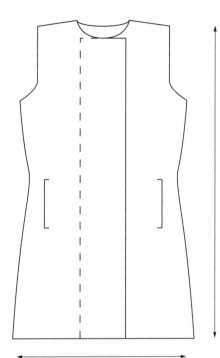

85 (86: 87: 88: 89: 90) cm
33 ½ (34: 34 ¼: 34 ¾: 35: 35 ½) in

44.5 (47: 49.5: 52: 55: 58.5) cm
17 ½ (18 ½: 19 ½: 20 ½: 21 ½: 23) in

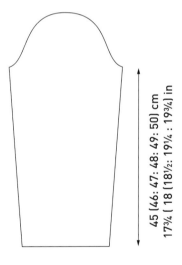

45 (46: 47: 48: 49: 50) cm
17¾ (18: 18½: 19¼: 19¾) in

BIANCA

Ribbed Sloppy Joe with flattering neck-line

Recommendation

Suitable for the knitter with a little experience
Please see pages 12 & 13 for photographs.

	XS	S	M	L	XL	XXL	
To fit	**81**	**86**	**91**	**97**	**102**	**109**	**cm**
bust	32	34	36	38	40	43	in

Rowan All Seasons Cotton

| | 16 | 17 | 19 | 21 | 23 | 25 | x 50gm |

Photographed in Bleached

Needles

1 pair 4mm (no 8) (US 6) needles
1 pair 4½mm (no 7) (US 7) needles

Tension

21 sts and 30 rows to 10 cm measured over
pattern using 4½mm (US 7) needles.

BACK and FRONT (both alike)

Cast on 113 (119: 125: 129: 135: 143) sts
using 4½mm (US 7) needles.
Row 1 (RS): K2 (1: 0: 2: 1: 1), P1, *K3, P1,
rep from * to last 2 (1: 0: 2: 1: 1) sts, K2 (1: 0:
2: 1: 1).
Row 2: K0 (0: 2: 0: 0: 0), P1 (0: 1: 1: 0: 0),
*K3, P1, rep from * to last 0 (3: 2: 0: 3: 3) sts,
K0 (3: 2: 0: 3: 3).
These 2 rows form patt.
Cont in patt until work measures 37 (37: 38:
38: 38: 38) cm, ending with a WS row.

Shape raglan armholes

Keeping patt correct, cast off 5 (4: 3: 5: 4: 4)
sts at beg of next 2 rows.
103 (111: 119: 119: 127: 135) sts.
Work 2 (2: 2: 2: 2: 0) rows, ending with a WS row.

Sizes XS, S and L only

Next row (RS): K1, P1, K3, P2tog, patt to
last 7 sts, P2tog tbl, K3, P1, K1.
Next row: K3, P1, K2, patt to last 6 sts, K2, P1, K3.
Next row: K1, P1, K3, P1, patt to last 6 sts,
P1, K3, P1, K1.
Next row: K3, P1, K2, patt to last 6 sts, K2, P1, K3.
Rep last 4 rows 5 (3: -: 2: -: -) times more.
91 (103: -: 113: -: -) sts.

Size XXL only

Next row (RS): K1, P1, K3, P2tog, patt to
last 7 sts, P2tog tbl, K3, P1, K1.
Next row: K3, P1, K1, K2tog tbl, patt to
last 7 sts, K2tog, K1, P1, K3. 131 sts.

All sizes

Next row (RS): K1, P1, K3, P2tog, patt to
last 7 sts, P2tog tbl, K3, P1, K1.
Next row: K3, P1, K2, patt to last 6 sts, K2, P1, K3.
Rep last 2 rows 19 (24: 32: 28: 35: 37) times,
ending with a WS row.
Cast off rem 51 (53: 53: 55: 55: 55) sts.

SLEEVES (both alike)

Cast on 97 (99: 101: 105: 107: 111) sts
using 4½mm (US 7) needles.
Beg with patt row 1, work in patt as given for
back and front until sleeve measures 14 (14:
15: 15: 16: 16) cm, ending with a WS row.

Shape raglan

Keeping patt correct, cast off 5 (4: 3: 5: 4: 4)
sts at beg of next 2 rows.
87 (91: 95: 95: 99: 103) sts.
Work 2 (0: 0: 2: 2: 2) rows, ending with a WS row.

Size M only

Next row (RS): K1, P1, K3, P2tog, patt to
last 7 sts, P2tog tbl, K3, P1, K1.
Next row: K3, P1, K1, K2tog tbl, patt to last
7 sts, K2tog, K1, P1, K3. 91 sts.

All sizes

Next row (RS): K1, P1, K3, P2tog, patt to
last 7 sts, P2tog tbl, K3, P1, K1.
Next row: K3, P1, K2, patt to last 6 sts, K2, P1, K3.
Rep last 2 rows 31 (33: 32: 34: 35: 37) times,
ending with a WS row.
Cast off rem 23 (23: 25: 25: 27: 27) sts.

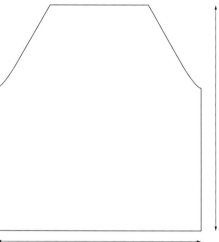
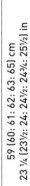

59 (60: 61: 62: 63: 65) cm
23 ¼ (23¾: 24: 24½: 24¾: 25½) in

54 (56.5: 59.5: 61.5: 64.5: 68) cm
21¼ (22¼: 23¼: 24¼: 25¼: 26½) in

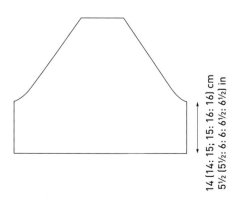

14 (14: 15: 15: 16: 16) cm
5½ (5½: 6: 6: 6½: 6½) in

Continued on next page...

SASSY
Crochet mesh poncho with fringing

Recommendation
Suitable for the novice
Please see pages 28, 29 & 52 for photographs.

	XS-S	M-L	XL-XXL	
To fit	**81-86**	**91-97**	**102-109**	**cm**
bust	32-34	36-38	40-43	**in**

Rowan Handknit Cotton
| | 4 | 6 | 8 | x 50gm |
Photographed in Bleached & Black

Crochet hook
4.00mm (no 8) (US G6) crochet hook

Tension
4 ch sps to 15 cm and 6 rows to 10 cm
measured over pattern using 4.00mm (US G6)
crochet hook.

Crochet abbreviations
ch = chain; **dc** = double crochet; **dtr** = double
treble; **sp(s)** = space(s); **ss** = slip stitch.

PONCHO (worked from neck downwards)
Make 110 (130: 150) ch using 4.00mm
(US G6) hook and join with a ss to form
a ring, taking care not to twist ch.
Round 1 (RS): 1 ch (does NOT count as st),
1 dc into each ch to end, ss to first dc, turn.
110 (130: 150) sts.
Now work in patt as folls:
Round 2: 1 ch (does NOT count as st),
1 dc into same place as ss at end of previous
round, *9 ch, miss 4 dc, 1 dc into next dc,
rep from * to last 4 dc, 5 ch, miss 4 dc,
1 dtr into top of dc at beg of round, turn.
22 (26: 30) ch sps.
Counting out from dc at beg of last round,
place markers on 5th (6th: 7th) and 6th
(7th: 8th) ch sps either side of this dc -
there will be 11 (13: 15) ch sps between
markers.
Round 3: 1 ch (does NOT count as st),
1 dc into ch sp partly formed by 5 ch at
end of previous round, *(9 ch, 1 dc into next
ch sp) until dc has been worked into marked
ch sp, 9 ch, 1 dc into same marked ch sp,
rep from * once more, (9 ch, 1 dc into next
ch sp) until dc has been worked into last
"empty" ch sp, 5 ch, 1 dtr into top of dc
at beg of round, turn.
24 (28: 32) ch sps.
Round 4: 1 ch (does NOT count as st), 1 dc
into ch sp partly formed by 5 ch at end of

previous round, (9 ch, 1 dc into next ch sp)
until dc has been worked into last "empty"
ch sp, 5 ch, 1 dtr into top of dc at beg of
round, turn.
Round 5: As round 4.
Round 6: 1 ch (does NOT count as st),
1 dc into ch sp partly formed by 5 ch at
end of previous round, *(9 ch, 1 dc into
next ch sp) until dc has been worked into
ch sp directly above marked ch sp, 9 ch,
1 dc into same ch sp, rep from * once
more, (9 ch, 1 dc into next ch sp) until
dc has been worked into last "empty"
ch sp, 5 ch, 1 dtr into top of dc at beg
of round, turn.
26 (30: 34) ch sps.
Rounds 7 to 18: As rounds 4 to 6, 4 times.
34 (38: 42) ch sps.
Now rep round 4, 4 (5: 6) times, ending
last round with "9 ch, ss to top of dc at beg
of round".
Fasten off.

MAKING UP
Press with a warm iron over a damp cloth.
Fringing
Cut 36 cm long lengths of yarn and knot
groups of 8 of these lengths through each
ch sp around lower edge of poncho to
form fringe.
Trim ends even.

BIANCA – Continued from previous page.

MAKING UP
Press all pieces with a warm iron over
a damp cloth.
Join all raglan seams using back stitch
or mattress stitch if preferred.
Collar
Cast on 177 (177: 185: 185: 193: 193) sts
using 4½mm (US 7) needles.
Row 1 (RS): P1, *K3, P1, rep from * to end.
Row 2: K2, P1, *K3, P1, rep from * to last
2 sts, K2.
These 2 rows form patt.

Cont in patt for a further 4 rows, ending
with a WS row.
Counting in from end of last row, place marker
on 19th st. Counting in from beg of last row,
place another marker on 71st (71st: 75th:
75th: 79th: 79th) st. There should be 87 (87:
91: 91: 95: 95) sts between marked sts.
Row 7 (dec) (RS): *Patt to within 2 sts of
marked st, work 2 tog, K marked st, work
2 tog tbl, rep from * once more, patt to end.
173 (173: 181: 181: 189: 189) sts.
Work 5 rows.

Rep last 6 rows 6 times more, then first
of these rows (the dec row) again.
145 (145: 153: 153: 161: 161) sts.
Change to 4mm (US 6) needles.
Cont in patt for a further 7 rows, ending with
a WS row.
Cast off.
Join row-end edges of collar.
Positioning marked sts centrally across
top of sleeves and collar seam near left back
raglan seam, sew cast-off edge of collar to
neck edge. Join side and sleeve seams.

Recommendation

Suitable for the more experienced knitter
Please see pages 32 & 33 for photographs.

	XS	S	M	L	XL	XXL	
To fit	**81**	**86**	**91**	**97**	**102**	**109**	cm
bust	32	34	36	38	40	43	in

Rowan Cotton Glace

7 7 8 8 9 10 x 50gm
Photographed in Dawn Grey

Needles

1 pair 2¾mm (no 12) (US 2) needles
1 pair 3¼mm (no 10) (US 3) needles

Buttons – 2

Extras – 170 cm of 4 cm wide ribbon

Tension

23 sts and 32 rows to 10 cm measured over
stocking stitch using 3¼mm (US 3) needles.

Special abbreviations

MP = make picot as folls: cast on 1 st, cast off
1 st - one st on right needle.

RITA
Neat cardigan with lace trims & ribbon tie

BACK
Lower back
Cast on 89 (95: 101: 107: 113: 121) sts using
3¼mm (US 3) needles.
Beg with a K row, work in st st for 4 rows,
ending with a WS row.
Next row (RS): K2, K2tog, K to last 4 sts,
K2tog tbl, K2.
Working all decreases as set by last row,
dec 1 st at each end of 4th and foll 4th row.
83 (89: 95: 101: 107: 115) sts.
Work 1 row, ending with a WS row.
Cast off.

Upper back
Cast on 83 (89: 95: 101: 107: 115) sts using
3¼mm (US 3) needles.
Beg with a K row, work in st st for 6 rows,
ending with a WS row.
Next row (RS): K2, M1, K to last 2 sts, M1, K2.
Working all increases as set by last row, inc
1 st at each end of 10th and 4 foll 10th rows.
95 (101: 107: 113: 119: 127) sts.
Work 7 (7: 11: 11: 11: 11) rows, ending with
a WS row.

Shape armholes
Cast off 3 (4: 4: 5: 5: 6) sts at beg of next
2 rows. 89 (93: 99: 103: 109: 115) sts.
Dec 1 st at each end of next 7 (7: 9: 9: 11:
11) rows, then on foll 2 (3: 3: 4: 4: 5) alt rows.
71 (73: 75: 77: 79: 83) sts.
Cont straight until armhole measures 17 (18:
18: 19: 20: 21) cm, ending with a WS row.

Shape shoulders and back neck
Cast off 7 (7: 7: 7: 7: 8) sts at beg of next
2 rows. 57 (59: 61: 63: 65: 67) sts.
Next row (RS): Cast off 7 (7: 7: 7: 7: 8) sts, K
until there are 10 (10: 11: 11: 12: 12) sts on right
needle and turn, leaving rem sts on a holder.
Work each side of neck separately.
Cast off 4 sts at beg of next row.
Cast off rem 6 (6: 7: 7: 8: 8) sts.
With RS facing, rejoin yarn to rem sts, cast off
centre 23 (25: 25: 27: 27: 27) sts, K to end.
Complete to match first side, reversing
shapings.

LEFT FRONT
Lower left front
Cast on 47 (50: 53: 56: 59: 63) sts using
3¼mm (US 3) needles.

Beg with a K row, work in st st for 4 rows,
ending with a WS row.
Working all decreases as set by back, dec
1 st at beg of next and 2 foll 4th rows.
44 (47: 50: 53: 56: 60) sts.
Work 1 row, ending with a WS row.
Cast off.

Upper left front
Cast on 44 (47: 50: 53: 56: 60) sts using
3¼mm (US 3) needles.
Beg with a K row, work in st st for 6 rows,
ending with a WS row.

Shape front slope
Next row (RS): K2, M1, K to last 4 sts, K2tog
tbl, K2.
Working all side seam increases and all front slope
decreases as set by last row, cont as folls:
Dec 1 st at front slope edge of 6th (4th: 6th: 4th:
6th: 6th) and 8 (8: 9: 9: 9: 9) foll 6th rows **and at
same time** inc 1 st at side seam of 10th and 4 foll
10th rows. 40 (43: 45: 48: 51: 55) sts.
Work 3 (5: 1: 3: 1: 1) rows, ending with
a WS row.

Shape armhole
Cast off 3 (4: 4: 5: 5: 6) sts at beg and dec
0 (1: 0: 0: 0: 0) st at end of next row.
37 (38: 41: 43: 46: 49) sts.
Work 1 row.
Dec 1 st at armhole edge of next 7 (7: 9: 9: 11:
11) rows, then on foll 2 (3: 3: 4: 4: 5) alt rows
and at same time dec 1 st at front slope edge
of next (5th: 3rd: next: 3rd: 3rd) and 1 (1: 2: 2:
2: 3) foll 6th rows. 26 (26: 26: 27: 28: 29) sts.
Dec 1 st at front slope edge **only** on 2nd (4th:
6th: 2nd: 2nd: 6th) and 5 (5: 3: 5: 4: 1) foll
6th rows, then on 0 (0: 1: 0: 1: 3) foll 8th rows.
20 (20: 21: 21: 22: 24) sts.
Cont straight until upper left front matches
upper back to start of shoulder shaping,
ending with a WS row.

Shape shoulder
Cast off 7 (7: 7: 7: 7: 8) sts at beg of next
and foll alt row.
Work 1 row.
Cast off rem 6 (6: 7: 7: 8: 8) sts.

RIGHT FRONT
Lower right front
Cast on 47 (50: 53: 56: 59: 63) sts using
3¼mm (US 3) needles.

Beg with a K row, work in st st for 4 rows, ending with a WS row.
Working all decreases as set by back, dec 1 st at end of next and 2 foll 4th rows.
44 (47: 50: 53: 56: 60) sts.
Work 1 row, ending with a WS row.
Cast off.

Upper right front
Cast on 44 (47: 50: 53: 56: 60) sts using 3¼mm (US 3) needles.
Beg with a K row, work in st st for 6 rows, ending with a WS row.

Shape front slope
Next row (RS): K2, K2tog, K to last 2 sts, M1, K2.
Working all side seam increases and all front slope decreases as set by last row, complete to match upper left front, reversing shapings.

SLEEVES (both alike)
First section
Using 2¾mm (US 2) needles work picot cast-on as folls: cast on 4 sts, cast off 1 st, slip st on right needle back onto left needle, *cast on 3 sts, cast off 1 st, slip st on right needle back onto left needle, rep from * until there are 31 (33: 33: 35: 35: 37) sts on left needle, cast on 1 (1: 1: 1: 2: 2) sts.
32 (34: 34: 36: 37: 39) sts.
Row 1 (RS): MP, K to end.
Row 2: Knit.
Rep last 2 rows twice more.
Change to 3¼mm (US 3) needles.
Row 7: MP, K to last 2 sts, M1, K2. 33 (35: 35: 37: 38: 40) sts.
Row 8: P to last 2 sts, K2.
Row 9: As row 1.
Row 10: As row 8.
Row 11: As row 1.
Shape top
Row 12 (WS): Cast off 3 (4: 4: 5: 5: 6) sts, P to last 2 sts, K2tog.
Break yarn and leave rem 29 (30: 30: 31: 32: 33) sts on a holder.
Second section
Using 2¾mm (US 2) needles work picot cast-on as folls: cast on 2 (2: 2: 2: 3: 3) sts, cast off 1 st, slip st on right needle back onto left needle, *cast on 3 sts, cast off 1 st, slip st on right needle back onto left needle, rep from * until there are 29 (31: 31: 33: 34: 36) sts on left needle, cast on 3 sts.
32 (34: 34: 36: 37: 39) sts.
Row 1 (RS): Knit.
Row 2: MP, K to end.
Rep last 2 rows twice more.
Change to 3¼mm (US 3) needles.

Row 7: K2, M1, K to end, K2.
33 (35: 35: 37: 38: 40) sts.
Row 8: MP, K until there are 2 sts on right needle, P to end.
Row 9: As row 1.
Row 10: As row 8.
Shape top
Row 11: Cast off 3 (4: 4: 5: 5: 6) sts, K to end.
Row 12 (WS): K2tog, P to end.
29 (30: 30: 31: 32: 33) sts.
Join sections
Next row (RS): K2tog, K next 27 (28: 28: 29: 30: 31) sts of second section, K first 27 (28: 28: 29: 30: 31) sts of first section, K2tog.
56 (58: 58: 60: 62: 64) sts.
Beg with a P row, cont in st st, dec 1 st at each end of next 2 rows, then on foll 2 alt rows, then on 5 foll 4th rows.
38 (40: 40: 42: 44: 46) sts.
Work 1 row, ending with a WS row.
Dec 1 st at each end of next and every foll alt row to 32 sts, then on foll 3 rows, ending with a WS row.
Cast off rem 26 sts.

MAKING UP
Press all pieces with a warm iron over a damp cloth.
Join side seams of upper sections, and of lower sections using back stitch or mattress stitch if preferred.
Waist insert panel (knitted sideways)
Cast on 9 sts using 3¼mm (US 3) needles.
Row 1 (RS): MP (one st on right needle), K1, (yfwd, K2tog) 3 times, K1.
Row 2: As row 1.
These 2 rows form patt.
Cont in patt until waist insert panel fits neatly along entire cast-on edge of upper fronts and back, ending with a WS row.
Cast off.
Lay picot edge of waist insert panel over cast-on edge of upper fronts and back as in photograph and neatly sew in place. In same way, lay other picot edge over cast-off edges of lower fronts and back and sew in place.
Hem border (knitted sideways)
Cast on 9 sts using 3¼mm (US 3) needles.
Row 1 (WS): K2, (yfwd, K2tog) twice, yfwd, K3. 10 sts.
Row 2 and every foll alt row: Knit.
Row 3: MP (one st on right needle), K1, (yfwd, K2tog) twice, yfwd, K4. 11 sts.
Row 5: K2, (yfwd, K2tog) twice, yfwd, K5. 12 sts.
Row 7: MP (one st on right needle), K1, (yfwd, K2tog) twice, yfwd, K6. 13 sts.
Row 9: K2, (yfwd, K2tog) twice, yfwd, K7. 14 sts.

Row 11: MP (one st on right needle), K1, (yfwd, K2tog) twice, yfwd, K8. 15 sts.
Row 12: Cast off 6 sts, K to end. 9 sts.
These 12 rows form patt.
Cont in patt until hem border fits neatly along entire cast-on edge of lower fronts and back, ending after patt row 12 and with a WS row.
Cast off.
Lay picot edge of hem border over cast-on edge of lower fronts and back as in photograph and neatly sew in place.
Join both shoulder seams.
Front band
Cast on 7 sts using 3¼mm (US 3) needles.
Row 1 (RS): MP, K to end.
Row 2: Knit.
These 2 rows form patt.
Cont in patt until front band, when slightly stretched, fits up entire right front opening edge, around back neck, then down entire left front opening edge, ending with a **RS** row.
Cast off knitwise (on **WS**).
Slip stitch front band neatly into position.
Join sleeve seams. Insert sleeves. Make button loops along front edge of sleeve opening as in photograph and attach buttons to correspond.
Using photograph as a guide, thread ribbon through waist insert panel and tie ends in a bow at centre front.

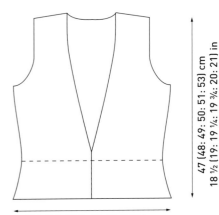

47 (48: 49: 50: 51: 53) cm
18 ½ (19: 19 ¼: 19 ¾: 20: 21) in

41.5 (44: 46.5: 49: 51.5: 55) cm
16½ (17½: 18¼: 19¼: 20¼: 21½) in

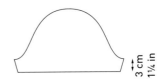

3 cm
1¼ in

Recommendation

Suitable for the knitter with a little experience
Please see pages 34 & 35 for photographs.

	XS	S	M	L	XL	XXL	
To fit	**81**	**86**	**91**	**97**	**102**	**109**	cm
bust	32	34	36	38	40	43	in

Rowan All Seasons Cotton

	15	16	17	19	20	22	x 50gm

Photographed in Bleached

Needles

1 pair 4mm (no 8) (US 6) needles
1 pair 4½mm (no 7) (US 7) needles
Cable needle

Tension

16 sts and 28 rows to 10 cm measured over
pattern using 4½mm (US 7) needles.

Special abbreviations

C8B = slip next 4 sts onto cn and leave
at back of work, K4, then K4 from cn;
C8F = slip next 4 sts onto cn and leave
at front of work, K4, then K4 from cn.

Pattern note: When casting off across top of
cables, dec 3 sts evenly across each cable. All
st counts given relate to original number of sts
and do NOT take into account these decreases.

DANIELA

Relaxed cabled & garter stitch belted cardigan

BACK

Cast on 75 (79: 83: 87: 91: 99) sts using
4½mm (US 7) needles.
Row 1 (RS): K3 (5: 7: 9: 11: 15), (yfrn,
P2tog, K5, yfrn, P2tog, K1, inc once in each
of next 3 sts, K1) twice, yfrn, P2tog, K9, yfrn,
P2tog, (K1, inc once in each of next 3 sts,
K1, yfrn, P2tog, K5, yfrn, P2tog) twice,
K3 (5: 7: 9: 11: 15).
87 (91: 95: 99: 103: 111) sts.
Now work in patt as folls:
Row 1 (WS): K3 (5: 7: 9: 11: 15), (yfrn, P2tog,
K5, yfrn, P2tog, P8) twice, yfrn, P2tog, K9, yfrn,
P2tog, (P8, yfrn, P2tog, K5, yfrn, P2tog) twice,
K3 (5: 7: 9: 11: 15).
Row 2: K3 (5: 7: 9: 11: 15), (yfrn, P2tog, K5,
yfrn, P2tog, K8) twice, yfrn, P2tog, K9, yfrn,
P2tog, (K8, yfrn, P2tog, K5, yfrn, P2tog) twice,
K3 (5: 7: 9: 11: 15).
Rows 3 to 10: As rows 1 and 2, 4 times.
Row 11: As row 1.
Row 12: K3 (5: 7: 9: 11: 15), (yfrn, P2tog, K5,
yfrn, P2tog, C8B) twice, yfrn, P2tog, K9, yfrn,
P2tog, (C8F, yfrn, P2tog, K5, yfrn, P2tog) twice,
K3 (5: 7: 9: 11: 15).
Rows 13 and 14: As rows 1 and 2.
These 14 rows form patt.
Cont in patt until back measures 44 (44: 45:
45: 45: 45) cm, ending with a WS row.
Shape armholes
Keeping patt correct, cast off 3 sts at beg
of next 2 rows. 81 (85: 89: 93: 97: 105) sts.
Dec 1 st at each end of next 3 (3: 5: 5: 7: 7)
rows, then on foll 1 (2: 1: 2: 1: 3) alt rows, then
on foll 4th row.
71 (73: 75: 77: 79: 83) sts.
Cont straight until armhole measures 28 (29:
29: 30: 31: 32) cm, ending with a WS row.
Shape back neck
Next row (RS): Patt 22 (22: 23: 23: 24: 26)
sts and turn, leaving rem sts on a holder.
Work each side of neck separately.
Keeping patt correct, dec 1 st at neck edge
of next row. 21 (21: 22: 22: 23: 25) sts.
Shape shoulder
Cast off 6 (6: 6: 6: 7: 7) sts at beg of next and
foll alt row (see pattern note) **and at same
time** dec 1 st at neck edge of next 3 rows.
Work 1 row.
Cast off rem 6 (6: 7: 7: 6: 8) sts.

With RS facing, rejoin yarn to rem sts, cast off
centre 27 (29: 29: 31: 31: 31) sts (see pattern
note), patt to end.
Complete to match first side, reversing
shapings.

LEFT FRONT

Cast on 45 (47: 49: 51: 53: 57) sts using
4½mm (US 7) needles.
Row 1 (RS): K3 (5: 7: 9: 11: 15), *yfrn, P2tog,
K5, yfrn, P2tog*, K1, inc once in each of next
3 sts, K1, rep from * to * once more, K5, P14.
48 (50: 52: 54: 56: 60) sts.
Now work in patt as folls:
Row 1 (WS): K19, *yfrn, P2tog, K5, yfrn,
P2tog*, P8, rep from * to * once more, K3 (5:
7: 9: 11: 15).
Row 2: K3 (5: 7: 9: 11: 15), *yfrn, P2tog, K5, yfrn,
P2tog*, K8, rep from * to * once more, K19.
Row 3: P14, K5, *yfrn, P2tog, K5, yfrn, P2tog*, P8,
rep from * to * once more, K3 (5: 7: 9: 11: 15).
Row 4: K3 (5: 7: 9: 11: 15), *yfrn, P2tog, K5, yfrn,
P2tog*, K8, rep from * to * once more, K5, P14.
Last 4 rows form ridge patt for 14 sts at front
opening edge.
Keeping ridge patt correct, cont as folls:
Row 5: Patt 14 sts, K5, *yfrn, P2tog, K5, yfrn,
P2tog*, P8, rep from * to * once more, K3 (5:
7: 9: 11: 15).
Row 6: K3 (5: 7: 9: 11: 15), *yfrn, P2tog, K5,
yfrn, P2tog*, K8, rep from * to * once more, K5,
patt 14 sts.
Rows 7 to 10: As rows 5 and 6, twice.
Row 11: As row 5.
Row 12: K3 (5: 7: 9: 11: 15), *yfrn, P2tog, K5,
yfrn, P2tog*, C8B, rep from * to * once more,
K5, patt 14 sts.
Rows 13 and 14: As rows 5 and 6.
Last 14 rows set the sts - front opening edge
14 sts in ridge patt with all other sts in patt
as for back.
Cont in patt until left front matches back to start
of armhole shaping, ending with a WS row.
Shape armhole
Keeping patt correct, cast off 3 sts at beg
of next row. 45 (47: 49: 51: 53: 57) sts.
Work 1 row.
Dec 1 st at armhole edge of next 3 (3: 5: 5: 7:
7) rows, then on foll 1 (2: 1: 2: 1: 3) alt rows,
then on foll 4th row. 40 (41: 42: 43: 44: 46) sts.

Cont straight until 56 (56: 56: 58: 58: 58)
rows less have been worked
than on back to start of shoulder shaping,
ending with a WS row.

Shape front slope
Next row (RS): Patt to last 16 sts, K2tog tbl,
patt 14 sts.
Working all front slope decreases as set by last
row, dec 1 st at front slope on 6th (6th: 6th:
4th: 4th: 4th) and 3 (7: 7: 1: 1: 1) foll 6th (6th:
6th: 4th: 4th: 4th) rows, then on 3 (-: -: 7: 7: 7)
foll 8th (-: -: 6th: 6th: 6th) rows.
32 (32: 33: 33: 34: 36) sts.
Work 7 rows, ending with a WS row.

Shape shoulder
Cast off 6 (6: 6: 6: 7: 7) sts at beg of next
and foll alt row, then 6 (6: 7: 7: 6: 8) sts at
beg of foll alt row (see pattern note).
Cont in ridge patt on rem 14 sts for a further
9.5 (10: 10: 10.5: 10.5: 10.5) cm (for back
neck border extension), ending with a WS row.
Cast off.

RIGHT FRONT
Cast on 45 (47: 49: 51: 53: 57) sts using
4½mm (US 7) needles.
Row 1 (RS): P14, K5, *yfrn, P2tog, K5, yfrn,
P2tog*, K1, inc once in each of next 3 sts,
K1, rep from * to * once more, K3 (5: 7: 9:
11: 15).
48 (50: 52: 54: 56: 60) sts.
Now work in patt as folls:
Row 1 (WS): K3 (5: 7: 9: 11: 15), *yfrn, P2tog,
K5, yfrn, P2tog*, P8, rep from * to * once more,
K19.
Row 2: K19, *yfrn, P2tog, K5, yfrn, P2tog*,
K8, rep from * to * once more, K3 (5: 7: 9:
11: 15).
Row 3: K3 (5: 7: 9: 11: 15), *yfrn, P2tog, K5, yfrn,
P2tog*, P8, rep from * to * once more, K5, P14.
Row 4: P14, K5, *yfrn, P2tog, K5, yfrn, P2tog*,
K8, rep from * to * once more, K3 (5: 7: 9:
11: 15).
Last 4 rows form ridge patt for 14 sts at front
opening edge.
Keeping ridge patt correct, cont as folls:
Row 5: K3 (5: 7: 9: 11: 15), *yfrn, P2tog, K5,
yfrn, P2tog*, P8, rep from * to * once more, K5,
patt 14 sts.
Row 6: Patt 14 sts, K5, *yfrn, P2tog, K5, yfrn,
P2tog*, K8, rep from * to * once more, K3 (5:
7: 9: 11: 15).
Rows 7 to 10: As rows 5 and 6, twice.
Row 11: As row 5.
Row 12: Patt 14 sts, K5, *yfrn, P2tog, K5, yfrn,
P2tog*, C8F, rep from * to * once more, K3 (5:
7: 9: 11: 15).

Rows 13 and 14: As rows 5 and 6.
Last 14 rows set the sts - front opening edge
14 sts in ridge patt with all other sts in patt
as for back.
Complete to match left front, reversing shapings
and working front slope shaping as folls:

Shape front slope
Next row (RS): Patt 14 sts, K2tog, patt to end.

SLEEVES (both alike)
Cast on 47 (49: 49: 51: 51: 53) sts using 4mm
(US 6) needles.
Row 1 (RS): K0 (0: 0: 0: 0: 1), P0 (1: 1: 2: 2:
2), *K2, P1, K2, P2, rep from * to last 5 (6: 6: 0:
0: 1) sts, (K2, P1) 1 (2: 2: 0: 0: 0) times, K2 (0:
0: 0: 0: 1).
Row 2: P0 (0: 0: 0: 0: 1), K0 (1: 1: 2: 2: 2),
*P2, K1, P2, K2, rep from * to last 5 (6: 6: 0: 0:
1) sts, (P2, K1) 1 (2: 2: 0: 0: 0) times, P2 (0: 0:
0: 0: 1).
These 2 rows form rib.
Rep these 2 rows until rib measures 5 (6: 6: 7:
7: 8) cm, ending with a RS row.
Next row (WS): Rib 8 (9: 9: 10: 10: 11), (M1,
rib 1) twice, M1, rib 27, M1, (rib 1, M1) twice, rib
8 (9: 9: 10: 10: 11).
53 (55: 55: 57: 57: 59) sts.
Change to 4½mm (US 7) needles.
Now work in patt as folls:
Row 1 (RS): Inc in first st, K4 (5: 5: 6: 6: 0),
(yfrn, P2tog, K5) 0 (0: 0: 0: 0: 1) times, yfrn,
P2tog, K8, (yfrn, P2tog, K5) 3 times, yfrn, P2tog,
K8, yfrn, P2tog, (K5, yfrn, P2tog) 0 (0: 0: 0: 0: 1)
times, K4 (5: 5: 6: 6: 0), inc in last st.
55 (57: 57: 59: 59: 61) sts.
Row 2: K6 (7: 7: 1: 1: 2), (yfrn, P2tog, K5) 0 (0:
0: 1: 1: 1) times, yfrn, P2tog, P8, (yfrn, P2tog, K5)
3 times, yfrn, P2tog, P8, yfrn, P2tog, (K5, yfrn,
P2tog) 0 (0: 0: 1: 1: 1) times, K6 (7: 7: 1: 1: 2).
Row 3: (Inc in first st) 0 (0: 0: 0: 1: 1) times,
K6 (7: 7: 1: 0: 1), (yfrn, P2tog, K5) 0 (0: 0: 1:
1: 1) times, yfrn, P2tog, K8, (yfrn, P2tog, K5)
3 times, yfrn, P2tog, K8, yfrn, P2tog, (K5, yfrn,
P2tog) 0 (0: 0: 1: 1: 1) times, K6 (7: 7: 1: 0: 1),
(inc in last st) 0 (0: 0: 0: 1: 1) times.
55 (57: 57: 59: 61: 63) sts.
Row 4: K6 (7: 7: 1: 2: 3), (yfrn, P2tog, K5)
0 (0: 0: 1: 1: 1) times, yfrn, P2tog, P8, (yfrn,
P2tog, K5) 3 times, yfrn, P2tog, P8, yfrn, P2tog,
(K5, yfrn, P2tog) 0 (0: 0: 1: 1: 1) times, K6 (7:
7: 1: 2: 3).
Row 5: Inc in first st, K5 (6: 6: 0: 1: 2), (yfrn,
P2tog, K5) 0 (0: 0: 1: 1: 1) times, yfrn, P2tog,
C8B, (yfrn, P2tog, K5) 3 times, yfrn, P2tog, C8F,
yfrn, P2tog, (K5, yfrn, P2tog) 0 (0: 0: 1:
1: 1) times, K5 (6: 6: 0: 1: 2), inc in last st.
57 (59: 59: 61: 63: 65) sts.

Row 6: K7 (1: 1: 2: 3: 4), (yfrn, P2tog, K5)
0 (1: 1: 1: 1: 1) times, yfrn, P2tog, P8, (yfrn,
P2tog, K5) 3 times, yfrn, P2tog, P8, yfrn, P2tog,
(K5, yfrn, P2tog) 0 (1: 1: 1: 1: 1) times, K7 (1:
1: 2: 3: 4).
Row 7: K7 (1: 1: 2: 3: 4), (yfrn, P2tog, K5)
0 (1: 1: 1: 1: 1) times, yfrn, P2tog, K8, (yfrn,
P2tog, K5) 3 times, yfrn, P2tog, K8, yfrn, P2tog,
(K5, yfrn, P2tog) 0 (1: 1: 1: 1: 1) times, K7 (1:
1: 2: 3: 4).
Row 8: As row 6.
Row 9: Inc in first st, K6 (0: 0: 1: 2: 3), (yfrn,
P2tog, K5) 0 (1: 1: 1: 1: 1) times, yfrn, P2tog,
K8, (yfrn, P2tog, K5) 3 times, yfrn, P2tog, K8,
yfrn, P2tog, (K5, yfrn, P2tog) 0 (1: 1: 1: 1: 1)
times, K6 (0: 0: 1: 2: 3), inc in last st.
59 (61: 61: 63: 65: 67) sts.

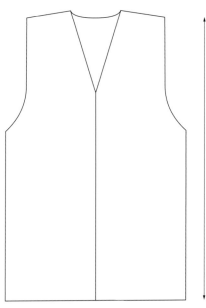

73 (74: 75: 76: 77: 78) cm
28¾ (29: 29½: 30: 30¼: 30¾) in

47 (49.5: 52: 54.5: 57: 61) cm
18 ½ (19½: 20½: 21½: 22½: 24) in

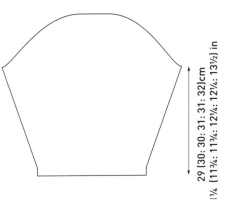

29 (30: 30: 31: 31: 32)cm
11¼ (11¾: 11¾: 12¼: 12¼: 13½) in

Continued on next page...

SIZZLE
T-shirt with wrap stitch detailing

Recommendation
Suitable for the knitter with a little experience
Please see pages 30 & 31 for photographs.

	XS	S	M	L	XL	XXL	
To fit	81	86	91	97	102	109	cm
bust	32	34	36	38	40	43	in

Rowan Pima Cotton
5	5	6	6	7	8	x 50gm

Photographed in Snow

Needles
1 pair 3¼mm (no 10) (US 3) needles
1 pair 3¾mm (no 9) (US 5) needles

Tension
20 sts and 27 rows to 10 cm measured over
pattern using 3¾mm (US 5) needles.

Special abbreviations
yrn2 = K1 winding yarn twice round needle;
yrn3 = K1 winding yarn 3 times round needle.

BACK and FRONT (both alike)
Cast on 92 (96: 102: 106: 112: 120) sts
using 3¼mm (US 3) needles.
Row 1 (RS): P0 (0: 0: 0: 0: 1), K0 (2: 0:
2: 0: 3), *P2, K3, rep from * to last 2 (4:
2: 4: 2: 1) sts, P2 (2: 2: 2: 2: 1), K0 (2:
0: 2: 0: 0).
Row 2: K0 (0: 0: 0: 0: 1), P0 (2: 0: 2:
0: 3), *K2, P3, rep from * to last 2 (4: 2:
4: 2: 1) sts, K2 (2: 2: 2: 2: 1), P0 (2: 0:
2: 0: 0).
These 2 rows form rib.
Work in rib for a further 27 rows, ending
with a **RS** row.
Change to 3¾mm (US 5) needles.
Beg and ending rows as indicated, repeating
the 40 row patt rep throughout and **noting**
that, unusually the chart as shown is the
wrong side of the fabric and chart row 1 is a
WS row, now work in patt from chart as folls:
Cont straight until work measures
22 (22: 23: 23: 23: 23) cm, ending
with a WS row.

Shape armholes
Keeping patt correct and noting that armhole
shaping is **NOT** shown on chart, cast off 6 sts
at beg of next 2 rows.
80 (84: 90: 94: 100: 108) sts.
Cont straight until armhole measures
18 (19: 19: 20: 21: 22) cm, ending
with a WS row.
Shape neck
Next row (RS): Patt 16 (17: 20: 21:
24: 28) sts and turn, leaving rem sts
on a holder.
Work each side of neck separately.
Keeping patt correct, dec 1 st at neck
edge of next 2 rows, then on foll alt row.
13 (14: 17: 18: 21: 25) sts.
Work 1 row, ending with a WS row.
Shape shoulder
Cast off 6 (7: 8: 9: 10: 12) sts at beg of
next row.
Work 1 row.
Cast off rem 7 (7: 9: 9: 11: 13) sts.
With RS facing, rejoin yarn to rem sts,
cast off centre 48 (50: 50: 52: 52: 52)
sts, patt to end.
Complete to match first side, reversing
shapings.

Continued on next page...

DANIELA – Continued from previous page.

Row 10: K1 (2: 2: 3: 4: 5), yfrn, P2tog, K5,
yfrn, P2tog, P8, (yfrn, P2tog, K5) 3 times, yfrn,
P2tog, P8, yfrn, P2tog, K5, yfrn, P2tog, K1 (2:
2: 3: 4: 5).
Row 11: K1 (2: 2: 3: 4: 5), yfrn, P2tog, K5,
yfrn, P2tog, K8, (yfrn, P2tog, K5) 3 times, yfrn,
P2tog, K8, yfrn, P2tog, K5, yfrn, P2tog, K1 (2:
2: 3: 4: 5).
Row 12: As row 10.
Row 13: Inc in first st, K0 (1: 1: 2: 3: 4), yfrn,
P2tog, K5, yfrn, P2tog, K8, (yfrn, P2tog, K5)
3 times, yfrn, P2tog, K8, yfrn, P2tog, K5, yfrn,
P2tog, K0 (1: 1: 2: 3: 4), inc in last st.
61 (63: 63: 65: 67: 69) sts.
Row 14: K2 (3: 3: 4: 5: 6), yfrn, P2tog, K5,
yfrn, P2tog, P8, (yfrn, P2tog, K5) 3 times, yfrn,
P2tog, P8, yfrn, P2tog, K5, yfrn, P2tog, K2 (3:
3: 4: 5: 6).
These 14 rows form patt and start sleeve shaping.

Cont in patt, inc 1 st at each end of 3rd and
every foll 4th row until there are 87 (89: 89:
91: 93: 95) sts, taking inc sts into patt.
Work 3 rows, ending with a WS row.
Shape top
Keeping patt correct, cast off 3 sts at beg
of next 2 rows.
81 (83: 83: 85: 87: 89) sts.
Work 2 rows, ending with a WS row.
Dec 1 st at each end of next and 4 foll 4th rows,
then on every foll alt row to 67 sts, then on foll
11 rows, ending with a WS row. 45 sts.
Cast off 3 sts at beg of next 4 rows (see pattern
note).
Cast off rem 33 sts.

MAKING UP
Press all pieces with a warm iron over
a damp cloth.

Join both shoulder seams using back stitch
or mattress stitch if preferred.
Join cast-off ends of back neck border
extensions, then sew one edge to back neck.
Join side seams. Join sleeve seams.
Insert sleeves.
Belt
Cast on 10 sts using 4mm (US 6) needles.
Row 1 (RS): Knit.
Rows 2 and 3: Purl.
Row 4: Knit.
These 4 rows form ridge patt.
Cont in ridge patt until belt measures approx
145 (150: 155: 160: 165: 170) cm, ending
after patt row 3 and with a **RS** row.
Cast off knitwise (on **WS**).
Try on jacket and mark position of waist.
Make belt loops at this level over side seams
and thread belt through loops.

SLEEVES (both alike)

Cast on 80 (84: 84: 88: 92: 96) sts using 3¼mm (US 3) needles.

Row 1 (RS): P1 (0: 0: 0: 0: 0), K3 (1: 1: 3: 0: 2), *P2, K3, rep from * to last 1 (3: 3: 0: 2: 4) sts, P1 (2: 2: 0: 2: 2), K0 (1: 1: 0: 0: 2).

Row 2: K1 (0: 0: 0: 0: 0), P3 (1: 1: 3: 0: 2), *K2, P3, rep from * to last 1 (3: 3: 0: 2: 4) sts, K1 (2: 2: 0: 2: 2), P0 (1: 1: 0: 0: 2).

These 2 rows form rib.

Work in rib for a further 17 rows, ending with a RS row.

Change to 3¾mm (US 5) needles.

Beg and ending rows as indicated, repeating the 40 row patt rep throughout and noting that chart row 1 is a WS row, now work in patt from chart as folls:

Cont straight until sleeve measures 14 (15: 15: 16: 17: 18) cm, ending with a WS row.

Cast off.

MAKING UP

Press all pieces with a warm iron over a damp cloth.

Join right shoulder seam using back stitch or mattress stitch if preferred.

Neckband

With RS facing and using 3¼mm (US 3) needles, pick up and knit 6 sts down left side of front neck, 48 (50: 50: 52: 52: 52) sts from front, 6 sts up right side of front neck, 6 sts down right side of back neck, 48 (50: 50: 52: 52: 52) sts from back, and 6 sts up left side of back neck. 120 (124: 124: 128: 128: 128) sts.

Beg with a K row, work in rev st st for 4 rows, ending with a RS row.

Cast off knitwise (on WS).

Join left shoulder and neckband seam. Join side seams. Join sleeve seams, leaving 3 cm open at underarm. Sew sleeves into armholes.

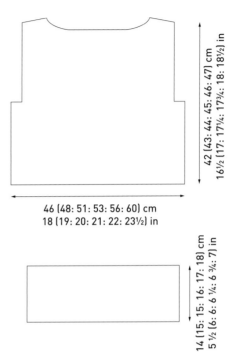

42 (43: 44: 45: 46: 47) cm
16½ (17: 17¼: 17¾: 18: 18½) in

46 (48: 51: 53: 56: 60) cm
18 (19: 20: 21: 22: 23½) in

14 (15: 15: 16: 17: 18) cm
5 ½ (6: 6: 6 ¼: 6 ¾: 7) in

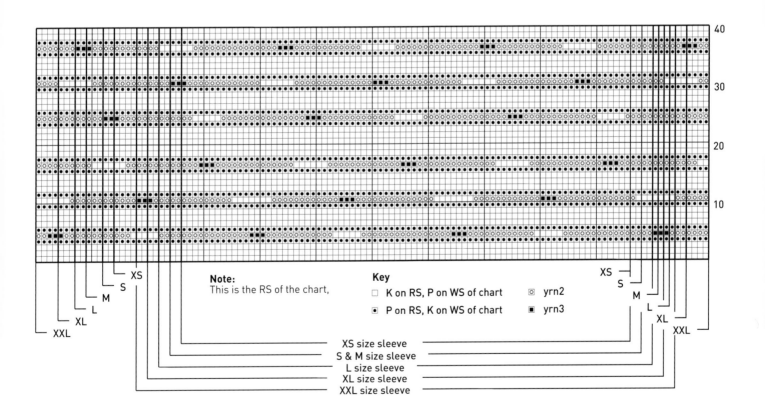

Note:
This is the RS of the chart,

Key

☐ K on RS, P on WS of chart   ⊙ yrn2

▪ P on RS, K on WS of chart   ▪ yrn3

XS size sleeve
S & M size sleeve
L size sleeve
XL size sleeve
XXL size sleeve

OBSESSION

Sassy cardigan with eyelet detail

Recommendation

Suitable for the knitter with a little experience
Please see pages 40 & 41 for photographs.

	XS	S	M	L	XL	XXL	
To fit	**81**	**86**	**91**	**97**	**102**	**109**	cm
bust	32	34	36	38	40	43	in

Rowan Siena 4 ply

	7	7	8	8	9	9	x 50gm

Photographed in Black

Needles

1 pair 2¼mm (no 13) (US 1) needles
1 pair 2¾mm (no 12) (US 2) needles

Buttons – 10

Tension

27 sts and 41 rows to 10 cm measured over
pattern using 2¾mm (US 2) needles.

BACK

Cast on 201 (213: 225: 243: 255: 279) sts
using 2¼mm (US 1) needles.
Row 1 (RS): K3, *cast off 3 sts, K until there
are 3 sts on right needle after cast-off, rep from
* to end. 102 (108: 114: 123: 129: 141) sts.
Work in g st for 5 rows, inc 1 (1: 1: 0: 0: 0) st at
beg of first of these rows and ending with a WS
row. 103 (109: 115: 123: 129: 141) sts.
Change to 2¾mm (US 2) needles.
Now work in patt as folls:
Beg with a K row, work in st st for 15 rows,
ending with a RS row.
Row 16 (WS): Knit.
Row 17: *K2tog, yfwd, rep from * to last st, K1.
Row 18: Knit.
These 18 rows form patt.
Cont in patt, dec 1 st at each end of next and 4
foll 6th rows. 93 (99: 105: 113: 119: 131) sts.
Work 23 rows, ending with a WS row.
Inc 1 st at each end of next and 4 foll 16th
rows, taking inc sts into patt.
103 (109: 115: 123: 129: 141) sts.
Work 11 (11: 15: 15: 15: 15) rows, ending
after patt row 16 (16: 2: 2: 2: 2) and with
a WS row. (Back should measure approx
37 (37: 38: 38: 38: 38) cm.)
Shape armholes
Keeping patt correct, cast off 4 (5: 5: 6: 6: 7)
sts at beg of next 2 rows.
95 (99: 105: 111: 117: 127) sts.
Dec 1 st at each end of next 3 (3: 5: 5: 7: 9)
rows, then on foll 1 (2: 2: 3: 3: 4) alt rows, then
on foll 4th row. 85 (87: 89: 93: 95: 99) sts.
Cont straight until armhole measures 17 (18:
18: 19: 20: 21) cm, ending with a WS row.
Shape shoulders and back neck
Cast off 5 (5: 5: 5: 6: 6) sts at beg of next
2 rows. 75 (77: 79: 83: 83: 87) sts.
Next row (RS): Cast off 5 (5: 5: 5: 6: 6) sts,
patt until there are 8 (8: 9: 10: 9: 11) sts on
right needle and turn, leaving rem sts on
a holder.
Work each side of neck separately.
Cast off 4 sts at beg of next row.
Cast off rem 4 (4: 5: 6: 5: 7) sts.
With RS facing, rejoin yarn to rem sts, cast off
centre 49 (51: 51: 53: 53: 53) sts, patt to end.
Complete to match first side, reversing
shapings.

LEFT FRONT

Cast on 117 (123: 129: 135: 141: 153) sts
using 2¼mm (US 1) needles.
Row 1 (RS): K3, *cast off 3 sts, K until there
are 3 sts on right needle after cast-off, rep from
* to end. 60 (63: 66: 69: 72: 78) sts.
Work in g st for 5 rows, dec 1 (1: 1: 0: 0: 0) st
at end of first of these rows and ending with
a WS row. 59 (62: 65: 69: 72: 78) sts.
Change to 2¾mm (US 2) needles.
Now work in patt as folls:
Row 1 (RS): Knit.
Row 2: K7, P to end.
Rows 3 to 14: As rows 1 and 2, 6 times.
Rows 15 and 16: Knit.
Row 17: *K2tog, yfwd, rep from * to last 7 (8:
7: 7: 8: 8) sts, K7 (8: 7: 7: 8: 8).
Row 18: Knit.
These 18 rows form patt and set the sts (front
opening edge 7 sts in g st with all other sts in
patt as given for back).
Cont in patt, dec 1 st at beg of next and 4 foll
6th rows. 54 (57: 60: 64: 67: 73) sts.
Work 23 rows, ending with a WS row.
Inc 1 st at beg of next and 4 foll 16th rows, taking
inc sts into patt. 59 (62: 65: 69: 72: 78) sts.
Work 11 (11: 15: 15: 15: 15) rows, ending
after patt row 16 (16: 2: 2: 2: 2) and with a WS
row. (Left front should measure approx 37 (37:
38: 38: 38: 38) cm.)
Shape armhole
Keeping patt correct, cast off 4 (5: 5: 6: 6: 7) sts
at beg of next rows.
55 (57: 60: 63: 66: 71) sts.
Work 1 row.
Dec 1 st at armhole edge of next 3 (3: 5: 5: 7:
9) rows, then on foll 1 (2: 2: 3: 3: 4) alt rows,
then on 1 (1: 1: 0: 1: 1) foll 4th row.
50 (51: 52: 55: 55: 57) sts.
Work 1 (3: 1: 3: 1: 1) rows, ending with a WS row.
Shape front neck
Next row (RS): (K2tog) 0 (0: 0: 1: 0: 0) times,
patt to last 20 (21: 21: 21: 21: 21) sts and
turn, leaving rem sts on a holder.
30 (30: 31: 33: 34: 36) sts.
Keeping patt correct, dec 1 st at neck edge
of next 8 rows, then on foll 4 alt rows, then on
1 (1: 1: 2: 2: 2) foll 4th rows, then on foll 6th
row, then on foll 8th row, then on foll 10th row.
14 (14: 15: 16: 17: 19) sts.

Cont straight until left front matches back to start of shoulder shaping, ending with a WS row.

Shape shoulder

Cast off 5 (5: 5: 5: 6: 6) sts at beg of next and foll alt row.

Work 1 row.

Cast off rem 4 (4: 5: 6: 5: 7) sts.

Mark positions for 10 buttons along left front opening edge - first button to come in row 5, last button to come just above neck shaping, and rem 8 buttons evenly spaced between.

RIGHT FRONT

Cast on 117 (123: 129: 135: 141: 153) sts using 2¼mm (US 1) needles.

Row 1 (RS): K3, *cast off 3 sts, K until there are 3 sts on right needle after cast-off, rep from * to end.

60 (63: 66: 69: 72: 78) sts.

Work in g st for 3 rows, dec 1 (1: 1: 0: 0: 0) st at beg of first of these rows and ending with a WS row.

59 (62: 65: 69: 72: 78) sts.

Row 5 (buttonhole row) (RS): K2, K2tog tbl, (yrn) twice, K2tog (to make a buttonhole - on next row work into front and back of double yrn), K to end.

Working a further 8 buttonholes in this way to correspond with positions marked for buttons on left front and noting that no further reference will be made to buttonholes, cont as folls:

Work in g st for 1 row more, ending with a WS row.

Change to 2¾mm (US 2) needles.

Now work in patt as folls:

Row 1 (RS): Knit.

Row 2: P to last 7 sts, K7.

Rows 3 to 14: As rows 1 and 2, 6 times.

Rows 15 and 16: Knit.

Row 17: K8 (7: 8: 8: 7: 7) (making buttonhole if appropriate), *K2tog, yfwd, rep from * to last st, K1.

Row 18: Knit.

These 18 rows form patt and set the sts (front opening edge 7 sts in g st with all other sts in patt as given for back).

Cont in patt, dec 1 st at end of next and 4 foll 6th rows. 54 (57: 60: 64: 67: 73) sts.

Complete to match left front, reversing shapings and working first row of neck shaping as folls:

Shape front neck

Next row (RS): Patt 20 (21: 21: 21: 21: 21) sts and slip these sts onto a holder, patt to last 0 (0: 0: 2: 0: 0) sts, (K2tog) 0 (0: 0: 1: 0: 0) times. 30 (30: 31: 33: 34: 36) sts.

SLEEVES (both alike)

Cast on 141 (153: 153: 159: 165: 171) sts using 2¼mm (US 1) needles.

Row 1 (RS): K3, *cast off 3 sts, K until there are 3 sts on right needle after cast-off, rep from * to end.

72 (78: 78: 81: 84: 87) sts.

Work in g st for 3 rows, inc (dec: dec: -: dec: -) 1 (1: 1: -: 1: -) st at centre of first of these rows and ending with a WS row.

73 (77: 77: 81: 83: 87) sts.

Inc 1 st at each end of next row.

75 (79: 79: 83: 85: 89) sts.

Work in g st for a further 3 rows, ending with a WS row.

Change to 2¾mm (US 2) needles.

Sizes XS and S only

Shape top

Next row (RS): Cast off 4 (5: -: -: -: -) sts (one st on right needle), *K2tog, yfwd, rep from * to last 2 (1: -: -: -: -) sts, K2 (1: -: -: -: -).

Next row: Cast off 4 (5: -: -: -: -) sts, K to end. 67 (69: -: -: -: -) sts.

Last 2 rows set position of patt as given for back.

Beg with 15 rows in st st, cont in patt as now set.

Sizes M, L, XL and XXL only

Next row (RS): *K2tog, yfwd, rep from * to last st, K1.

Next row: Knit.

Last 2 rows set position of patt as given for back.

Beg with 15 rows in st st, cont in patt as now set.

Work 2 rows, ending with a WS row.

Shape top

Keeping patt correct, cast off - (-: 5: 6: 6: 7) sts at beg of next 2 rows. - (-:69: 71: 73: 75) sts.

All sizes

Keeping patt correct, cont as folls:

Dec 1 st at each end of next 3 rows, then on foll alt row, then on foll 4th row, then on 4 foll 6th rows.

49 (51: 51: 53: 55: 57) sts.

Work 3 rows, ending with a WS row.

Dec 1 st at each end of next and every foll alt row to 39 sts, then on foll 3 rows, ending with a WS row. 33 sts.

Cast off 3 sts at beg of next 2 rows.

Cast off rem 27 sts.

MAKING UP

Press all pieces with a warm iron over a damp cloth.

Join both shoulder seams using back stitch or mattress stitch if preferred.

Neckband

With RS facing and using 2¼mm (US 1) needles, slip 20 (21: 21: 21: 21: 21) sts from right front holder onto right needle, rejoin yarn and pick up and knit 42 (42: 42: 46: 46: 46) sts up right side of neck, 57 (59: 59: 61: 61: 61) sts from back, and 42 (42: 42: 46: 46: 46) sts down left side of neck, then patt across 20 (21: 21: 21: 21: 21) sts on left front holder. 181 (185: 185: 195: 195: 195) sts.

Work in g st for 4 rows, making 10th buttonhole in 2nd of these rows and ending with a **RS** row.

Cast off knitwise (on **WS**).

Join side seams. Join sleeve seams.

Insert sleeves. Sew on buttons.

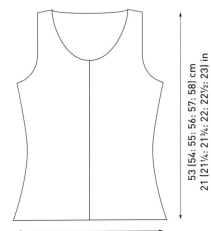

53 (54: 55: 56: 57: 58) cm
21 (21¼: 21¾: 22: 22½: 23) in

38 (40: 42.5: 45.5: 48: 52) cm
15 (15¾: 16¾: 18: 19: 20½) in

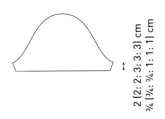

2 (2: 2: 3: 3: 3) cm
¾ (¾: ¾: 1: 1: 1) in

GABRIELA

Sweet cropped cabled cardigan

Recommendation
Suitable for the knitter with a little experience
Please see pages 38 & 39 for photographs.

	XS	S	M	L	XL	XXL	
To fit	**81**	**86**	**91**	**97**	**102**	**109**	cm
bust	32	34	36	38	40	43	in

Rowan Sienna 4 ply
8	9	9	10	10	11	x 50gm

Photographed in Bleached

Needles
1 pair 2¼mm (no 13) (US 1) needles
1 pair 2¾mm (no 12) (US 2) needles
Cable needle

Buttons – 9

Tension
27 sts and 44 rows to 10 cm measured over
pattern using 2¾mm (US 2) needles.

Special abbreviations
C4B = slip next 2 sts onto cn and leave at back
of work, K2, then K2 from cn;
C4F = slip next 2 sts onto cn and leave at front
of work, K2, then K2 from cn.

BACK
Cast on 87 (93: 99: 107: 111: 123) sts using
2¼mm (US 1) needles.
Row 1 (RS): K1 (0: 1: 1: 0: 0), *P1, K1, rep from *
to last 0 (1: 0: 0: 1: 1) st, P0 (1: 0: 0: 1: 1).
Row 2: P1 (0: 1: 1: 0: 0), *K1, P1, rep from *
to last 0 (1: 0: 0: 1: 1) st, K0 (1: 0: 0: 1: 1).
These 2 rows form rib.
Cont in rib for a further 21 rows, inc 1 st at each
end of 17th row and ending with a **RS** row.
89 (95: 101: 109: 113: 125) sts.
Row 24 (WS): Rib 2 (5: 8: 12: 2: 8), (M1, rib
12) 3 (3: 3: 3: 4: 4) times, M1, rib 13, M1, (rib
12, M1) 3 (3: 3: 3: 4: 4) times, rib 2 (5: 8: 12:
2: 8).
97 (103: 109: 117: 123: 135) sts.
Change to 2¾mm (US 2) needles.
Beg and ending rows as indicated and
repeating the 12 row patt rep throughout,
now work in patt from chart as folls:
Inc 1 st at each end of 11th and 3 foll
16th rows, taking inc sts into patt.
105 (111: 117: 125: 131: 143) sts.
Cont straight until back measures 22 (22: 23:
23: 23: 23) cm, ending with a WS row.
Shape armholes
Keeping patt correct, cast off 4 (5: 5: 6: 6: 7)
sts at beg of next 2 rows.
97 (101: 107: 113: 119: 129) sts.
Dec 1 st at each end of next 3 (3: 5: 5: 7: 9)
rows, then on foll 2 (3: 3: 4: 4: 5) alt rows, then
on 2 foll 4th rows.
83 (85: 87: 91: 93: 97) sts.
Cont straight until armhole measures 17 (18:
18: 19: 20: 21) cm, ending with a WS row.
Shape shoulders and back neck
Cast off 7 (7: 7: 8: 8: 9) sts at beg of next
2 rows.
69 (71: 73: 75: 77: 79) sts.
Next row (RS): Cast off 7 (7: 7: 8: 8: 9) sts,
patt until there are 11 (11: 12: 11: 12: 12)
sts on right needle and turn, leaving rem
sts on a holder.
Work each side of neck separately.
Cast off 4 sts at beg of next row.
Cast off rem 7 (7: 8: 7: 8: 8) sts.
With RS facing, rejoin yarn to rem sts, cast off
centre 33 (35: 35: 37: 37: 37) sts dec 2 sts at
top of each of centre 2 cables, patt to end.
Complete to match first side, reversing shapings.

LEFT FRONT
Cast on 49 (52: 55: 59: 61: 67) sts using
2¼mm (US 1) needles.
Row 1 (RS): K1 (0: 1: 1: 1: 1), *P1, K1, rep
from * to last 8 sts, K8.
Row 2: K8, P1, *K1, P1, rep from * to last 0 (1:
0: 0: 0: 0) st, K0 (1: 0: 0: 0: 0).
These 2 rows set the sts - front opening edge
8 sts in g st with all other sts in rib.
Cont as set for a further 21 rows, inc 1 st at
beg of 17th row and ending with a **RS** row.
50 (53: 56: 60: 62: 68) sts.
Row 24 (WS): K8, rib 4, M1, (rib 12, M1) 3 (3:
3: 3: 4: 4) times, rib 2 (5: 8: 12: 2: 8).
54 (57: 60: 64: 67: 73) sts.
Change to 2¾mm (US 2) needles.
Beg and ending rows as indicated and
repeating the 12 row patt rep throughout,
now work in patt from chart as folls:
Row 1 (RS): Work first 46 (49: 52: 56: 59: 65)
sts as row 1 of chart, K8.
Row 2: K8, work rem 46 (49: 52: 56: 59: 65)
sts as row 2 of chart.
These 2 rows set the sts - front opening edge
8 sts still in g st with all other sts now in patt
from chart.
Keeping sts correct as now set, cont as folls:
Inc 1 st at beg of 9th and 3 foll 16th rows,
taking inc sts into patt.
58 (61: 64: 68: 71: 77) sts.
Cont straight until left front matches back
to start of armhole shaping, ending with
a WS row.
Shape armhole
Keeping patt correct, cast off 4 (5: 5: 6: 6: 7)
sts at beg of next row.
54 (56: 59: 62: 65: 70) sts.
Work 1 row.
Dec 1 st at armhole edge of next 3 (3: 5: 5: 7:
9) rows, then on foll 2 (3: 3: 4: 4: 5) alt rows,
then on 2 foll 4th rows.
47 (48: 49: 51: 52: 54) sts.
Cont straight until 28 (28: 28: 32: 32: 32) rows
less have been worked than on back
to start of shoulder shaping, ending with
a WS row.
Shape front neck
Next row (RS): Patt 31 (31: 32: 34: 35: 37)
sts and turn, leaving rem 16 (17: 17: 17: 17:
17) sts on a holder.

Keeping patt correct, dec 1 st at neck edge
of next 6 rows, then on foll 2 alt rows, then
on 1 (1: 1: 2: 2: 2) foll 4th rows, then on foll
6th row.
21 (21: 22: 23: 24: 26) sts.
Work 7 rows, ending with a WS row.

Shape shoulder
Cast off 7 (7: 7: 8: 8: 9) sts at beg of next row.
Work 1 row.
Cast off rem 7 (7: 8: 7: 8: 8) sts.
Mark positions for 9 buttons along left
front opening edge - first button to come
in row 5, last button to come level with
neck shaping, and rem 7 buttons evenly
spaced between.

RIGHT FRONT
Cast on 49 (52: 55: 59: 61: 67) sts using
2¼mm (US 1) needles.
Row 1 (RS): K9, *P1, K1, rep from * to last
0 (1: 0: 0: 0: 0) st, P0 (1: 0: 0: 0: 0).
Row 2: P1 (0: 1: 1: 1: 1), *K1, P1, rep from *
to last 8 sts, K8.
These 2 rows set the sts - front opening edge
8 sts in g st with all other sts in rib.
Cont as set for a further 2 rows, ending with
a WS row.
Row 5 (buttonhole row) (RS): K2, K2tog tbl,
(yrn) twice, K2tog (to make a buttonhole - on
next row work twice into double yrn
of previous row), K2, rib to end.
Working a further 7 buttonholes in this way
to correspond with positions marked for
buttons on left front and noting that no
further reference will be made to buttonholes,
cont as folls:
Work 18 rows, inc 1 st at end of 14th row
and ending with a RS row.
50 (53: 56: 60: 62: 68) sts.
Row 24 (WS): Rib 2 (5: 8: 12: 2: 8),
M1, (rib 12, M1) 3 (3: 3: 3: 4: 4) times,
rib 4, K8.
54 (57: 60: 64: 67: 73) sts.
Change to 2¾mm (US 2) needles.
Beg and ending rows as indicated and
repeating the 12 row patt rep throughout,
now work in patt from chart as folls:
Row 1 (RS): K8, work rem 46 (49: 52: 56:
59: 65) sts as row 1 of chart.
Row 2: Work first 46 (49: 52: 56: 59: 65) sts
as row 2 of chart, K8.
These 2 rows set the sts - front opening edge
8 sts still in g st with all other sts now in patt
from chart.
Complete to match left front, reversing
shapings and working first row of neck
shaping as folls:

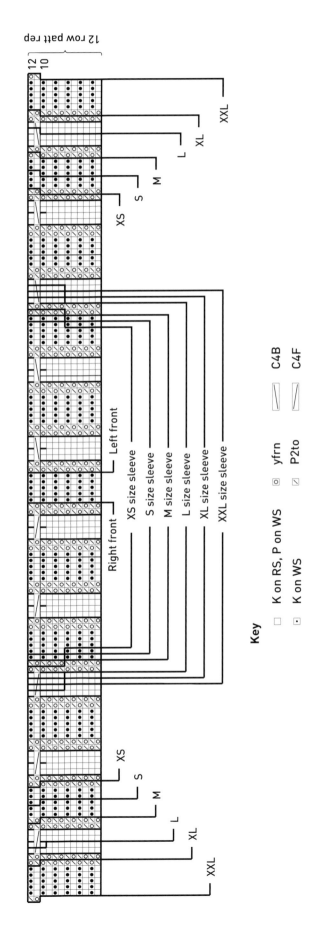

Key

☐	K on RS, P on WS
·	K on WS

| ⊙ | yfrn |
| ◩ | P2to |

| ╲ | C4B |
| ╱ | C4F |

Shape front neck

Next row (RS): K2, K2tog tbl, (yrn) twice, K2tog (to make 9th buttonhole - on next row work twice into double yrn of previous row), K2, patt 2 sts, (K2tog) twice, patt 2 (3: 3: 3: 3: 3) sts and slip these 14 (15: 15: 15: 15: 15) sts onto a holder, patt to end.
31 (31: 32: 34: 35: 37) sts.

SLEEVES (both alike)

Cast on 47 (49: 51: 55: 57: 59) sts using 2¼mm (US 1) needles.

Row 1 (RS): K1, *P1, K1, rep from * to end.
Row 2: P1, *K1, P1, rep from * to end.
These 2 rows form rib.
Cont in rib for a further 21 rows, inc 1 st at each end of 17th row and ending with a **RS** row.
49 (51: 53: 57: 59: 61) sts.
Row 24 (WS): Rib 6 (7: 8: 10: 11: 12), (M1, rib 12) 3 times, M1, rib 7 (8: 9: 11: 12: 13).
53 (55: 57: 61: 63: 65) sts.
Change to 2¾mm (US 2) needles.
Beg and ending rows as indicated and repeating the 12 row patt rep throughout, now work in patt from chart as folls:
Inc 1 st at each end of 7th and every foll 10th (10th: 10th: 12th: 12th: 12th) row to 65 (63: 61: 85: 83: 81) sts, then on every foll 12th (12th: 12th: 14th: 14th: 14th) row until there are 81 (83: 85: 89: 91: 93) sts, taking inc sts into patt.
Cont straight until sleeve measures 45 (46: 47: 48: 49: 50) cm, ending with a WS row.

Shape top

Keeping patt correct, cast off 4 (5: 5: 6: 6: 7) sts at beg of next 2 rows.
73 (73: 75: 77: 79: 79) sts.
Dec 1 st at each end of next 3 rows, then on foll alt row, then on foll 4th row, then on 4 foll 6th rows.
55 (55: 57: 59: 61: 61) sts.
Work 3 rows, ending with a WS row.
Dec 1 st at each end of next and foll 4th row, then on foll 2 (4: 3: 4: 5: 7) alt rows, then on foll 9 (7: 9: 9: 9: 7) rows, ending with a WS row.
Cast off rem 29 sts.

MAKING UP

Press all pieces with a warm iron over a damp cloth.
Join both shoulder seams using back stitch or mattress stitch if preferred.

Neckband

With RS facing and using 2¼mm (US 1) needles, slip 14 (15: 15: 15: 15: 15) sts from right front holder onto right needle, rejoin yarn

and pick up and knit 30 (30: 30: 34: 34: 34) sts up right side of neck, 33 (35: 35: 37: 37: 37) sts from back, and 30 (30: 30: 34: 34: 34) sts down left side of neck, then patt across 16 (17: 17: 17: 17: 17) sts on left front holder as folls: patt 2 (3: 3: 3: 3: 3) sts, (K2tog) twice, patt to end. 121 (125: 125: 135: 135: 135) sts.
Work in g st for 6 rows, ending with a RS row.
Cast off knitwise (on **WS**).
Join side seams. Join sleeve seams. Insert sleeves. Sew on buttons.

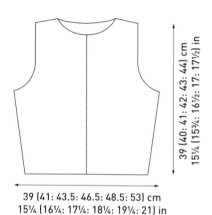

39 (41: 43.5: 46.5: 48.5: 53) cm
15¼ (16¼: 17¼: 18¼: 19¼: 21) in

39 (40: 41: 42: 43: 44) cm
15¼ (15¾: 16¼: 16½: 17: 17½) in

45 (46: 47: 48: 49: 50) cm
17¾ (18: 18½: 19: 19¼: 19¾) in

MARSHA
Lace edged garter stitch cardigan

Recommendation
Suitable for the more experienced knitter
Please see pages 48 & 49 for photographs.

	XS	S	M	L	XL	XXL	
To fit	**81**	**86**	**91**	**97**	**102**	**109**	cm
bust	32	34	36	38	40	43	in

Rowan Pima Cotton
	11	12	13	14	15	16	x 50gm

Photographed in Millett

Needles
1 pair 3mm (no 11) (US 2/3) needles
1 pair 3¼mm (no 10) (US 3) needles

Tension
25 sts and 44 rows to 10 cm measured over
garter stitch using 3¼mm (US 3) needles.

BACK
Cast on 105 (111: 117: 125: 131: 141) sts
using 3mm (US 2/3) needles.
Work in g st for 8 rows, ending with a WS row.
Change to 3¼mm (US 3) needles.
Work in g st for a further 12 rows, ending with
a WS row.
Shape waist darts
Counting in from both ends of last row, place
markers on 24th (25th: 27th: 29th: 30th:
32nd) st in from both ends of row.
Next row (dec) (RS): K3, K2tog, *K to within
3 sts of marked st, K2tog, K3 (marked st is
centre st of these 3 sts), K2tog tbl, rep from
* once more, K to last 5 sts, K2tog tbl, K3.
99 (105: 111: 119: 125: 135) sts.
Work 15 rows.
Rep last 16 rows once more, then first of these
rows (the dec row) again.
87 (93: 99: 107: 113: 123) sts.
Work 35 rows, ending with a WS row.
Next row (inc) (RS): K3, M1, *K to within
1 st of marked st, M1, K3 (marked st is centre
st of these 3 sts), M1, rep from * once more,
K to last 3 sts, M1, K3.
93 (99: 105: 113: 119: 129) sts.
Work 25 rows.
Rep last 26 rows once more, then first of these
rows (the inc row) again.
105 (111: 117: 125: 131: 141) sts.
Work 27 (27: 31: 31: 35: 35) rows, ending with
a WS row. (Back should measure
38 (38: 39: 39: 40: 40) cm.)
Shape armholes
Cast off 4 (5: 5: 6: 6: 7) sts at beg of next
2 rows. 97 (101: 107: 113: 119: 127) sts.
Dec 1 st at each end of next 3 (3: 5: 5: 7: 7)
rows, then on foll 5 (5: 4: 5: 4: 6) alt rows, then
on 2 foll 4th rows.
77 (81: 85: 89: 93: 97) sts.
Cont straight until armhole measures 16 (17:
17: 18: 18: 19) cm, ending with a WS row.
Shape back neck
Next row (RS): K25 (26: 28: 30: 32: 34)
and turn, leaving rem sts on a holder.
Work each side of neck separately.
Dec 1 st at neck edge of next 4 rows, then
on foll alt row.
20 (21: 23: 25: 27: 29) sts.
Work 1 row, ending with a WS row.

Shape shoulder
Cast off 6 (7: 7: 8: 9: 9) sts at beg of next and
foll alt row and at same time dec 1 st at neck
edge of next row.
Work 1 row.
Cast off rem 7 (6: 8: 8: 8: 10) sts.
With RS facing, rejoin yarn to rem sts, cast off
centre 27 (29: 29: 29: 29: 29) sts, K to end.
Complete to match first side, reversing
shapings.

LEFT FRONT
Cast on 53 (56: 59: 63: 66: 71) sts using
3mm (US 2/3) needles.
Row 1 (RS): K to last 15 (15: 15: 20: 20:
20) sts, place marker on right needle, work
last 15 (15: 15: 20: 20: 20) sts as row 1 of
appropriate chart for left front.
Row 2: Work row 2 of appropriate chart
for left front, slip marker onto right needle,
K to end.
These 2 rows set the sts - front opening edge
sts beyond marker in patt from chart for left
front with all other sts in g st.
Working appropriate rows of chart and repeating
the 16 row patt rep throughout, cont as folls:
(**Note:** Marker just placed will **NOT** be
referred to again until beg of front slope
shaping. Number of sts in patt beyond
marker varies whilst working chart but
all st counts given presume there are
15 (15: 15: 20: 20: 20) sts beyond
marker at all times.)
Work 6 rows, ending with a WS row.
Change to 3¼mm (US 3) needles.
Work 12 rows, ending with a WS row.
Shape waist darts
Counting in from end of last row, place dart
marker on 24th (25th: 27th: 29th: 30th:
32nd) st in from end of row.
Next row (dec) (RS): K3, K2tog, K to within
3 sts of marked dart st, K2tog, K3 (marked
st is centre st of these 3 sts), K2tog tbl,
patt to end.
50 (53: 56: 60: 63: 68) sts.
Work 15 rows.
Rep last 16 rows once more, then first of
these rows (the dec row) again.
44 (47: 50: 54: 57: 62) sts.
Work 29 rows, ending with a WS row.

Shape front slope

Next row (RS): K to within 2 sts of chart marker, K2tog tbl, slip chart marker onto right needle, patt to end. 43 (46: 49: 53: 56: 61) sts. Working all front slope shaping as set by last row, cont as folls:

Work 5 rows, ending with a WS row.

Next row (inc) (RS): K3, M1, K to within 1 st of marked dart st, M1, K3 (marked st is centre st of these 3 sts), M1, patt to end.
46 (49: 52: 56: 59: 64) sts.

Working dart and side seam increases as set by last row (3 increased sts on each inc row), cont as folls:

Dec 1 st at front slope edge of 24th and 1 (1: 1: 1: 2: 2) foll 30th rows **and at same time** inc 3 sts (at side seam and dart) on 26th and foll 26th row. 50 (53: 56: 60: 62: 67) sts.

Work 25 (25: 29: 29: 3: 3) rows, ending with a WS row.

Shape armhole

Keeping patt correct, cast off 4 (5: 5: 6: 6: 7) sts at beg and dec 0 (0: 1: 1: 0: 0) st at front slope edge of next row.
46 (48: 50: 53: 56: 60) sts.
Work 1 row.

Dec 1 st at armhole edge of next 3 (3: 5: 5: 7: 7) rows, then on foll 5 (5: 4: 5: 4: 6) alt rows, then on 2 foll 4th rows **and at same time** dec 1 (1: 0: 0: 0: 1) st at front slope edge of 3rd (3rd: 0: 0: 0: 25th) row. 35 (37: 39: 41: 43: 44) sts.

Dec 1 st at front slope edge only on 12th (12th: 8th: 6th: 2nd: 28th) and 0 (1: 1: 1: 1: 0) foll 30th row. 34 (35: 37: 39: 41: 43) sts. Cont straight until left front matches back to beg of shoulder shaping, ending with a WS row.

Shape shoulder

Cast off 6 (7: 7: 8: 9: 9) sts at beg of next and foll alt row, then 7 (6: 8: 8: 8: 10) sts at beg of foll alt row.

Cont in patt as set on rem 15 sts for a further 7.5 (8: 8: 8: 8: 8) cm (for back neck border extension), ending with a **RS** row.

Cast off (on **WS**).

RIGHT FRONT

Cast on 53 (56: 59: 63: 66: 71) sts using 3mm (US 2/3) needles.

Row 1 (RS): Work first 15 (15: 15: 20: 20: 20) sts as row 1 of appropriate chart for right front, place marker on right needle, K to end.

Row 2: K to marker, slip marker onto right needle, work row 2 of appropriate chart for right front.

These 2 rows set the sts - front opening edge sts beyond marker in patt from chart for right front with all other sts in g st.

Working appropriate rows of chart and repeating the 16 row patt rep throughout, cont as folls:

(**Note:** Marker just placed will **NOT** be referred to again until beg of front slope shaping.

Number of sts in patt beyond marker varies whilst working chart but all st counts given presume there are 15 (15: 15: 20: 20: 20) sts beyond marker at all times.)

Work 6 rows, ending with a WS row. Change to 3¼mm (US 3) needles. Work 12 rows, ending with a WS row.

Shape waist darts

Counting in from beg of last row, place dart marker on 24th (25th: 27th: 29th: 30th: 32nd) st in from end of row.

Next row (dec) (RS): Patt to within 3 sts of marked dart st, K2tog, K3 (marked st is centre st of these 3 sts), K2tog tbl, K to last 5 sts, K2tog tbl, K3.
50 (53: 56: 60: 63: 68) sts.
Work 15 rows.
Rep last 16 rows once more, then first of these rows (the dec row) again.
44 (47: 50: 54: 57: 62) sts.
Work 29 rows, ending with a WS row.

Shape front slope

Next row (RS): Patt to chart marker, slip chart marker onto right needle, K2tog, K to end.
43 (46: 49: 53: 56: 61) sts.
Working all front slope shaping as set by last row, complete to match left front, reversing shapings.

Key

☐ K on RS, P on WS	☑ K2tog
⊡ P on RS, K on WS	◩ K2tog tbl
◎ Yon	⊍ K3tog
	◤ K3tog tbl

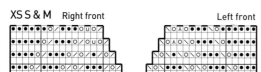

XS S & M   Right front   Left front   16 / 10

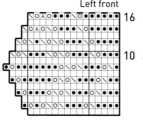

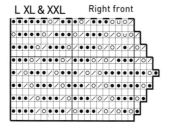

L XL & XXL   Right front   Left front   16 / 10

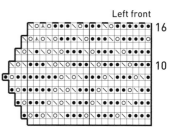

SLEEVES (both alike)

Cast on 48 (50: 50: 52: 56: 58) sts using 3mm (US 2/3) needles.

Work in g st for 12 rows, ending with a WS row. Change to 3¼mm (US 3) needles.

Row 13 (inc) (RS): K3, M1, K to last 3 sts, M1, K3.

Working all increases as set by last row, inc 1 st at each end of 12th (12th: 12th: 12th: 14th: 14th) and every foll 12th (12th: 12th: 12th: 14th: 14th) row to 72 (70: 66: 64: 72: 86) sts, then on every foll 14th (14th: 14th: 14th: 16th: -) row until there are 76 (78: 78: 80: 82: -) sts.

Cont straight until sleeve measures 45 (46: 47: 48: 49: 50) cm, ending with a WS row.

Shape top

Cast off 4 (5: 5: 6: 6: 7) sts at beg of next 2 rows. 68 (68: 68: 68: 70: 72) sts.

Dec 1 st at each end of next 3 rows, then on foll 3 alt rows, then on 3 (2: 2: 2: 2: 2) foll 4th rows. 50 (52: 52: 52: 54: 56) sts.

Work 5 rows, ending with a WS row.

Dec 1 st at each end of next and 1 (3: 3: 4: 4: 4) foll 6th rows, then on 2 (2: 2: 1: 1: 1) foll 4th rows, then on every foll alt row to 30 sts, then on foll row, ending with a WS row.

Cast off rem 28 sts.

MAKING UP

Press all pieces with a warm iron over a damp cloth.

Join both shoulder seams using back stitch or mattress stitch if preferred. Join cast-off edges of back neck border extensions, then sew one edge to back neck.

Join side seams. Join sleeve seams. Sew sleeves into armholes.

42 (44.5: 47: 50: 52.5: 56.5) cm
16½ (17½: 18½: 19¾: 20¾: 22¼) in

56 (57: 58: 59: 60: 61) cm
22 (22½: 22¾: 23¼: 23½: 24) in

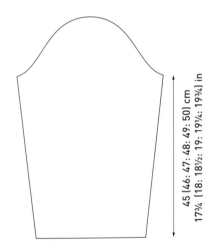

45 (46: 47: 48: 49: 50) cm
17¾ (18: 18½: 19: 19¼: 19¾) in

EBONY

Skimming tunic worked in an open stitch

Recommendation

Suitable for the novice knitter
Please see pages 43, 44 & 45 for photographs.

	XS	S	M	L	XL	XXL	
To fit	81	86	91	97	102	109	cm
bust	32	34	36	38	40	43	in

Rowan Handknit Cotton

| | 8 | 9 | 9 | 10 | 10 | 11 | x 50gm |

Photographed in Black

Needles

1 pair 4mm (no 8) (US 6) needle
1 pair 8mm (no 0) (US 11) needles

Tension

12½ sts and 20 rows to 10 cm measured over pattern using a combination of 4mm (US 6) and 8mm (US 11) needles.

BACK and FRONT (both alike)

Cast on 55 (59: 63: 65: 69: 73) sts using 8mm (US 11) needles.
Now work in patt as folls:
Row 1 (RS): Using a 4mm (US 6) needle, knit.
Row 2: Using an 8mm (US 11) needle, purl.
These 2 rows form patt.
Keeping patt correct throughout, using 4mm (US 6) needle for all RS rows and 8mm (US 11) needle for all WS rows, cont as folls:
Work 34 rows, ending with a WS row.
Row 37 (RS): K3, K2tog, K to last 5 sts, K2tog tbl, K3.
Working all decreases as set by last row, dec 1 st at each end of 8th and 4 foll 6th rows. 43 (47: 51: 53: 57: 61) sts.
Cont straight until work measures 43 (43: 44: 44: 44: 44) cm, ending with a WS row.
Next row (RS): K3, M1, K to last 3 sts, M1, K3.
Working all increases as set by last row, inc 1 st at each end of 8th and foll 8th row, then on foll 6th row.
51 (55: 59: 61: 65: 69) sts.
Work 5 rows, ending with a WS row.
Shape armholes
Keeping patt correct, cast off 2 (3: 3: 4: 4: 5) sts at beg of next 2 rows.
47 (49: 53: 53: 57: 59) sts.
Dec 1 st at each end of next 1 (1: 3: 3: 3: 3) rows, then on foll 2 (2: 1: 1: 2: 2) alt rows, then on foll 4th row.
39 (41: 43: 43: 45: 47) sts.
Cont straight until armhole measures 18 (19: 19: 20: 21: 22) cm, ending with a WS row.
Shape shoulders and neck
Cast off 2 (2: 3: 2: 3: 4) sts at beg of next row.
Next row (WS): Cast off first 2 (2: 3: 2: 3: 4) sts purlwise, cast off rem 35 (37: 37: 39: 39: 39) sts knitwise.
Place marker 2 (2: 3: 2: 3: 4) sts in from beg of cast-off row (to denote other side of neck opening).

SLEEVES (both alike)

Cast on 25 (27: 29: 29: 31: 31) sts using 8mm (US 11) needles.
Now work in patt as folls:

Row 1 (RS): Using a 4mm (US 6) needle, knit.
Row 2: Using an 8mm (US 11) needle, purl.
These 2 rows form patt.

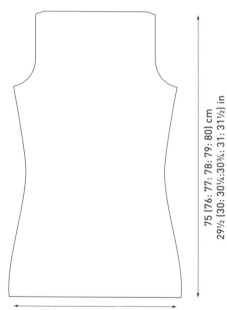

41 (44: 47: 49: 52: 55) cm
16¼ (17¼: 18½: 19¼: 2½: 21¾) in

75 (76: 77: 78: 79: 80) cm
29½ (30: 30¼:30¾: 31: 31½) in

48 (49: 50: 51: 52: 53) cm
19 (19¼: 19¾: 20: 20½: 21) in

Continued on next page...

Recommendation

Suitable for the knitter with a little experience
Please see page 47 for photograph.

One size

Rowan All Seasons Cotton

        2   x 50gm
Photographed in Black

Needles

1 pair 3¾mm (no 9) (US 5) needles
1 pair 4½mm (no 7) (US 7) needles

Tension

15½ sts and 28 rows to 10 cm measured over
pattern using 4½mm (US 7) needles.

JOLE
Slightly slouchy textured hat

HAT

Cast on 74 sts using 3¾mm (US 5) needles.
Row 1 (RS): K2, *P2, K2, rep from * to end.
Row 2: P2, *K2, P2, rep from * to end.
These 2 rows form rib.
Work in rib for a further 11 rows, ending with
a RS row.
Row 14 (WS): P2, *(K2, P2) twice, K2, P1, M1, P1,
rep from * to last 12 sts, (K2, P2) 3 times. 79 sts.
Change to 4½mm (US 7) needles.
Now work in patt as folls:
Row 1 (RS): K1, *K2, yfwd, K8, yfwd, K3, rep
from * to end. 91 sts.
Row 2: K1, *K3, P8, K4, rep from * to end.
Row 3: K1, *K3, yfwd, K8, yfwd, K4, rep from *
to end. 103 sts.
Row 4: K1, *K4, P8, K5, rep from * to end.
Row 5: K1, *K4, yfwd, K8, yfwd, K5, rep from *
to end. 115 sts.
Row 6: K1, *K5, P8, K6, rep from * to end.
Row 7: K1, *K5, K4tog tbl, K4tog, K6, rep from
* to end. 79 sts.
Row 8: Knit.
These 8 rows form patt.
Cont in patt for a further 24 rows, ending with
a WS row.

Shape top

Row 1 (RS): K1, *K2tog tbl, yfwd, K8, yfwd,
K2tog, K1, rep from * to end.
79 sts.
Row 2: K1, *K2, P8, K3, rep from * to end.
Row 3: K1, *K2, yfwd, K8, yfwd, K3, rep from *
to end. 91 sts.
Row 4: K1, *K3, P8, K4, rep from * to end.
Row 5: K1, *K3, yfwd, K8, yfwd, K4, rep from *
to end. 103 sts.
Row 6: K1, *K4, P8, K5, rep from * to end.
Row 7: K1, *K2tog tbl, K2, K4tog tbl, K4tog,
K2, K2tog, K1, rep from * to end. 55 sts.
Rows 8 to 10: Knit.
Row 11: K1, *K2tog tbl, K4, K2tog, K1, rep
from * to end. 43 sts.
Row 12: Knit.
Row 13: K1, *K2tog tbl, K2, K2tog, K1, rep
from * to end. 31 sts.
Row 14: Knit.
Row 15: K1, *K2tog tbl, K2tog, K1, rep from *
to end. 19 sts.
Row 16: K1, (K2tog) 9 times.
Break yarn and thread through rem 10 sts.
Pull up tight and fasten off securely.
Join back seam.

EBONY – *Continued from previous page.*

Keeping patt correct throughout, using
4mm (US 6) needle for all RS rows and 8mm
(US 11) needle for all WS rows, cont as folls:
Work 16 rows, ending with a WS row.
Working all increases in same way as side
seam increases, inc 1 st at each end of
next and every foll 10th (10th: 12th: 10th:
10th: 8th) row to 31 (31: 43: 41: 41: 35)
sts, then on every foll 12th (12th: -: 12th:
12th: 10th) row until there are 39 (41: -:
45: 47: 49) sts.

Cont straight until sleeve measures 48 (49:
50: 51: 52: 53) cm, ending with a WS row.
Shape top
Keeping patt correct, cast off 2 (3: 3: 4: 4: 5)
sts at beg of next 2 rows.
35 (35: 37: 37: 39: 39) sts.
Dec 1 st at each end of next and foll
alt row, then on 3 (4: 4: 4: 4: 4) foll
4th rows.
25 (23: 25: 25: 27: 27) sts.
Work 1 row.

Dec 1 st at each end of next and foll 2 (1: 0:
2: 1: 3) alt rows, then on foll 3 (3: 5: 3: 5: 3)
rows, ending with a WS row.
Cast off rem 13 sts.

MAKING UP
Press all pieces with a warm iron over a damp
cloth.
Join both shoulder seams using back stitch or
mattress stitch if preferred.
Join side seams. Join sleeve seams. Insert sleeves.

PALOMA

Wide sweater with wrap stitch detail

BACK and FRONT (both alike)

Cast on 122 (128: 134: 140: 146: 154) sts using 3¼mm (US 3) needles.

Beg with a K row, work in st st for 5 rows, ending with a **RS** row.

Change to 3¾mm (US 5) needles.

Row 6 (WS): Knit.

Row 7: K to end, winding yarn twice round needle for every st.

Row 8: K to end, dropping extra loops.

Beg with a K row, work in st st for 5 rows, ending with a **RS** row.

Rows 14 to 16: As rows 6 to 8.

Beg with a K row, work in st st for 7 rows, ending with a **RS** row.

Rows 24 to 26: As rows 6 to 8.

These 26 rows complete border.

Now work in patt as folls:

Beg with a K row, work in st st for 8 rows, ending with a WS row.

Row 9 (RS): K to end, winding yarn twice round needle for every st.

Row 10: P to end, dropping extra loops.

These 10 rows form patt.

Cont in patt until work measures 49 (50: 51: 52: 53: 54) cm, ending with a WS row.

Shape neck

Next row (RS): Patt 26 (28: 31: 33: 36: 40) sts and turn, leaving rem sts on a holder.

Work each side of neck separately.

Keeping patt correct, dec 1 st at neck edge of next row, ending with a WS row.

25 (27: 30: 32: 35: 39) sts.

Shape shoulder

Cast off 8 (8: 9: 10: 11: 12) sts at beg and dec 1 st at end of next row.

Work 1 row.

Rep last 2 rows once more.

Cast off rem 7 (9: 10: 10: 11: 13) sts.

With RS facing, rejoin yarn to rem sts, cast off centre 70 (72: 72: 74: 74: 74) sts, patt to end.

Complete to match first side, reversing shapings.

SLEEVES (both alike)

Cast on 50 (52: 54: 56: 58: 60) sts using 3¼mm (US 3) needles.

Beg with a K row, work in st st for 5 rows, ending with a **RS** row.

Change to 3¾mm (US 5) needles.

Row 6 (WS): Knit.

Row 7: K to end, winding yarn twice round needle for every st.

Recommendation

Suitable for the knitter with a little experience
Please see pages 50 & 51 for photographs.

	XS	S	M	L	XL	XXL	
To fit	81	86	91	97	102	109	cm
bust	32	34	36	38	40	43	in

Rowan Lenpur Linen

7 8 9 10 11 13 x 50gm

Photographed in Tattoo

Needles

1 pair 2¾mm (no 12) (US 2) needles
1 pair 3¼mm (no 10) (US 3) needles
1 pair 3¾mm (no 9) (US 5) needles

Tension

22 sts and 28 rows to 10 cm measured over pattern using 3¾mm (US 5) needles.

49 (50: 51: 52: 53: 54) cm
19¼ (19¾: 20: 21½: 21: 21¼) in

25 (26: 27: 28: 29: 30) cm
10 (10¼: 10½: 11: 11¾) in

55.5 (58: 61: 63.5: 66.5: 70) cm
22 (23: 24: 25: 26: 27½) in

Continued on next page...

CHRISTINA

Cardigan in pretty textured stripes

Recommendation

Suitable for the knitter with a little experience
Please see pages 10 & 11 for photographs.

	XS	S	M	L	XL	XXL	
To fit	**81**	**86**	**91**	**97**	**102**	**109**	cm
bust	32	34	36	38	40	43	in

Rowan Cotton Glace

| | 10 | 11 | 11 | 12 | 12 | 13 | x 50gm |

Photographed in Bleached

Needles

1 pair 2¾mm (no 12) (US 2) needles
1 pair 3¼mm (no 10) (US 3) needles

Buttons – 9

Tension

24 sts and 39 rows to 10 cm measured over
pattern using 3¼mm (US 3) needles.

BACK

Cast on 189 (201: 213: 225: 237: 255) sts
using 2¾mm (US 2) needles.
Row 1 (RS): K3, *cast off 3 sts, K until there
are 3 sts on right needle after cast-off, rep
from * to end.
96 (102: 108: 114: 120: 129) sts.
Rows 2 to 6: Knit, dec 1 (1: 1: 1: 1: 0) st at end
of last row. 95 (101: 107: 113: 119: 129) sts.
Change to 3¼mm (US 3) needles.
Row 7: Purl.
Row 8: Knit.
Row 9: Purl.
Row 10 (WS): K3 (2: 5: 4: 3: 4), yfrn, P1,
yon, *K3, yfrn, P1, yon, rep from * to last
3 (2: 5: 4: 3: 4) sts, K3 (2: 5: 4: 3: 4).
Row 11: P3 (2: 5: 4: 3: 4), K3, *P3, K3, rep
from * to last 3 (2: 5: 4: 3: 4) sts, P3 (2: 5:
4: 3: 4).
Row 12: K3 (2: 5: 4: 3: 4), P3, *K3, P3, rep from
* to last 3 (2: 5: 4: 3: 4) sts, K3 (2: 5: 4: 3: 4).
Row 13: As row 11.
Row 14: K3 (2: 5: 4: 3: 4), P3tog, *K3, P3tog,
rep from * to last 3 (2: 5: 4: 3: 4) sts, K3 (2: 5:
4: 3: 4).
Rows 15 and 16: As rows 7 and 8.
These 16 rows complete border.
Beg and ending rows as indicated and
repeating the 54 row patt rep throughout,
now work in patt from chart as folls:

Dec 1 st at each end of 7th and 3 foll
6th rows. 87 (93: 99: 105: 111: 121) sts.
Work 19 rows, ending with a WS row.
Inc 1 st at each end of next and 4 foll
14th rows, taking inc sts into patt.
97 (103: 109: 115: 121: 131) sts.
Work 13 (13: 17: 17: 17: 17) rows, ending
after patt row 6 (6: 10: 10: 10: 10) and
with a WS row.

Shape armholes

Keeping patt correct, cast off 3 (4: 4: 5: 5: 6)
sts at beg of next 2 rows.
91 (95: 101: 105: 111: 119) sts.
Dec 1 st at each end of next 5 (5: 7: 7: 9: 11)
rows, then on foll 1 (2: 2: 3: 2: 3) alt rows, then
on 2 foll 4th rows. 75 (77: 79: 81: 85: 87) sts.
Cont straight until armhole measures 18 (19:
19: 20: 21: 22) cm, ending with a WS row.

Shape shoulders and back neck

Cast off 7 (7: 7: 7: 8: 8) sts at beg of next 2 rows.
61 (63: 65: 67: 69: 71) sts.
Next row (RS): Cast off 7 (7: 7: 7: 8: 8) sts, patt
until there are 10 (10: 11: 11: 11: 12) sts on right
needle and turn, leaving rem sts on a holder.
Work each side of neck separately.
Cast off 4 sts at beg of next row.
Cast off rem 6 (6: 7: 7: 7: 8) sts.
With RS facing, rejoin yarn to rem sts, cast off
centre 27 (29: 29: 31: 31: 31) sts, patt to end.
Complete to match first side, reversing shapings.

Continued on next page...

PALOMA – *Continued from previous page.*

Row 8: K to end, dropping extra loops.
These 8 rows complete border.
Now work in patt as folls:
Beg with a K row, work in st st for 8 rows, inc
1 st at each end of next and foll 6th row and
ending with a WS row.
54 (56: 58: 60: 62: 64) sts.
Row 9 (RS): K to end, winding yarn twice
round needle for every st.
Row 10: P to end, dropping extra loops.
These 10 rows form patt and beg sleeve
shaping.
Cont in patt, shaping sides by inc 1 st at each
end of 3rd and 3 (4: 5: 7: 8: 10) foll 6th rows,

then on 7 (6: 5: 3: 2: 0) foll 4th rows.
76 (78: 80: 82: 84: 86) sts.
Work 5 rows, ending with a WS row. (Sleeve
should measure 25 (26: 27: 28: 29: 30) cm.)
Cast off.

MAKING UP

Press all pieces with a warm iron over
a damp cloth.
Join right shoulder seam using back stitch
or mattress stitch if preferred.

Neckband

With RS facing and using 2¾mm (US 2)
needles, pick up and knit 6 sts down left side

of front neck, 70 (72: 72: 74: 74: 74) sts from
front, 6 sts up right side of front neck, 6 sts
down right side of back neck, 70 (72: 72: 74:
74: 74) sts from back, and 6 sts up left side
of back neck.
164 (168: 168: 172: 172: 172) sts.
Beg with a K row, work in rev st st for 4 rows,
ending with a **RS** row.
Cast off knitwise (on **WS**).
Join left shoulder and neckband seam. Mark
points along side seams 17 (17.5: 18: 18.5:
19: 19.5) cm either side of shoulder seams
and sew sleeves to back and front between
these points. Join side and sleeve seams.

LEFT FRONT

Cast on 105 (111: 117: 123: 129: 141) sts using 2¾mm (US 2) needles.

Row 1 (RS): K3, *cast off 3 sts, K until there are 3 sts on right needle after cast-off, rep from * to end. 54 (57: 60: 63: 66: 72) sts.

Rows 2 to 6: Knit, dec 0 (0: 0: 0: 0: 1) st at end of last row. 54 (57: 60: 63: 66: 71) sts. Change to 3¼mm (US 3) needles.

Row 7: P to last 6 sts, K6.

Row 8: Knit.

Row 9: P to last 6 sts, K6.

Row 10 (WS): K10, yfrn, P1, yon, *K3, yfrn, P1, yon, rep from * to last 3 (2: 5: 4: 3: 4) sts, K3 (2: 5: 4: 3: 4).

Row 11: P3 (2: 5: 4: 3: 4), K3, *P3, K3, rep from * to last 10 sts, P4, K6.

Row 12: K10, P3, *K3, P3, rep from * to last 3 (2: 5: 4: 3: 4) sts, K3 (2: 5: 4: 3: 4).

Row 13: As row 11.

Row 14: K10, P3tog, *K3, P3tog, rep from * to last 3 (2: 5: 4: 3: 4) sts, K3 (2: 5: 4: 3: 4).

Rows 15 and 16: As rows 7 and 8.

These 16 rows complete border.

Beg and ending rows as indicated and repeating the 54 row patt rep throughout, now work in patt from chart as folls:

Row 1 (RS): Work first 48 (51: 54: 57: 60: 65) sts as row 1 of chart, K6.

Row 2: K6, work rem 48 (51: 54: 57: 60: 65) sts as row 2 of chart.

These 2 rows set the sts - front opening edge 6 sts in g st with all other sts in patt from chart.

Keeping sts correct as now set, cont as folls:
Dec 1 st at beg of 5th and 3 foll 6th rows. 50 (53: 56: 59: 62: 67) sts.

Work 19 rows, ending with a WS row.

Inc 1 st at beg of next and 4 foll 14th rows, taking inc sts into patt. 55 (58: 61: 64: 67: 72) sts.

Work 13 (13: 17: 17: 17: 17) rows, ending after patt row 6 (6: 10: 10: 10: 10) and with a WS row.

Shape armhole

Keeping patt correct, cast off 3 (4: 4: 5: 5: 6) sts at beg of next row. 52 (54: 57: 59: 62: 66) sts.

Work 1 row.

Dec 1 st at armhole edge of next 5 (5: 7: 7: 9: 11)

rows, then on foll 1 (2: 2: 3: 2: 3) alt rows, then on 2 foll 4th rows. 44 (45: 46: 47: 49: 50) sts.

Cont straight until 24 (24: 24: 28: 28: 28) rows less have been worked than on back to start of shoulder shaping, ending with a WS row.

Shape front neck

Next row (RS): Patt 32 (32: 33: 34: 36: 37) sts and turn, leaving rem 12 (13: 13: 13: 13: 13) sts on a holder.

Keeping patt correct, dec 1 st at neck edge of next 6 rows, then on foll 4 alt rows, then on 2 (2: 2: 3: 3: 3) foll 4th rows. 20 (20: 21: 21: 23: 24) sts.

Work 1 row, ending with a WS row.

Key

☐ K on RS, P on WS

▣ P on RS, K on WS

◉ yfwd on RS, yrn on WS

◪ K2tog on RS, P2tog on WS

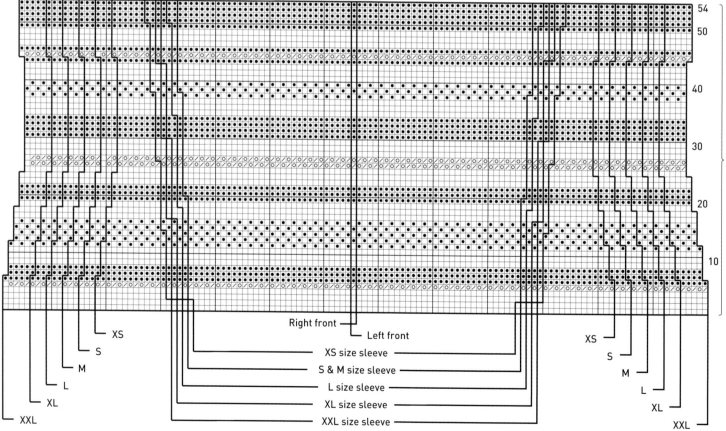

54 row patt rep

Right front — Left front

XS size sleeve

S & M size sleeve

L size sleeve

XL size sleeve

XXL size sleeve

XS · S · M · L · XL · XXL

XS · S · M · L · XL · XXL

Shape shoulder

Cast off 7 (7: 7: 7: 8: 8) sts at beg of next row. Work 1 row.

Cast off rem 6 (6: 7: 7: 7: 8) sts.

Mark positions for 9 buttons along left front opening edge - first button to come level with chart row 7, last button to come just above neck shaping, and rem 7 buttons evenly spaced between.

RIGHT FRONT

Cast on 105 (111: 117: 123: 129: 141) sts using 2¾mm (US 2) needles.

Row 1 (RS): K3, *cast off 3 sts, K until there are 3 sts on right needle after cast-off, rep from * to end. 54 (57: 60: 63: 66: 72) sts.

Rows 2 to 6: Knit, dec 0 (0: 0: 0: 0: 1) st at beg of last row. 54 (57: 60: 63: 66: 71) sts.

Change to 3¼mm (US 3) needles.

Row 7: K6, P to end.

Row 8: Knit.

Row 9: K6, P to end.

Row 10 (WS): K3 (2: 5: 4: 3: 4), yfrn, P1, yon, *K3, yfrn, P1, yon, rep from * to last 10 sts, K10.

Row 11: K6, P4, K3, *P3, K3, rep from * to last 3 (2: 5: 4: 3: 4) sts, P3 (2: 5: 4: 3: 4).

Row 12: K3 (2: 5: 4: 3: 4), P3, *K3, P3, rep from * to last 10 sts, K10.

Row 13: As row 11.

Row 14: K3 (2: 5: 4: 3: 4), P3tog, *K3, P3tog, rep from * to last 10 sts, K10.

Rows 15 and 16: As rows 7 and 8.

These 16 rows complete border.

Change to 3¼mm (US 3) needles.

Beg and ending rows as indicated and repeating the 54 row patt rep throughout, now work in patt from chart as folls:

Row 1 (RS): K6, work rem 48 (51: 54: 57: 60: 65) sts as row 1 of chart.

Row 2: Work first 48 (51: 54: 57: 60: 65) sts as row 2 of chart, K6.

These 2 rows set the sts - front opening edge 6 sts in g st with all other sts in patt from chart.

Keeping sts correct as now set, cont as folls:

Work 4 rows, ending with a WS row.

Next row (buttonhole row) (RS): K1, K2tog tbl, (yrn) twice, K2tog (to make a buttonhole - on next row work twice into double yrn of previous row), patt to last 2 sts, P2tog.

Working a further 7 buttonholes in this way to correspond with positions marked for buttons on left front and noting that no further reference will be made to buttonholes, complete to match left front, reversing shapings and working first row of neck shaping as folls:

Shape front neck

Next row (RS): Patt 12 (13: 13: 13: 13: 13) sts and slip these sts onto a holder, patt to end. 32 (32: 33: 34: 36: 37) sts.

SLEEVES (both alike)

Cast on 117 (117: 117: 123: 129: 129) sts using 2¾mm (US 2) needles.

Row 1 (RS): K3, *cast off 3 sts, K until there are 3 sts on right needle after cast-off, rep from * to end. 60 (60: 60: 63: 66: 66) sts.

Rows 2 to 6: Knit, dec (inc: inc: -: dec: inc) 1 (1: 1: 1: -: 1: 1) st at end of last row. 59 (61: 61: 63: 65: 67) sts.

Change to 3¼mm (US 3) needles.

Row 7: Purl.

Row 8: Knit.

Row 9: Purl.

Row 10 (WS): K3 (4: 4: 5: 2: 3), yfrn, P1, yon, *K3, yfrn, P1, yon, rep from * to last 3 (4: 4: 5: 2: 3) sts, K3 (4: 4: 5: 2: 3).

Row 11: P3 (4: 4: 5: 2: 3), K3, *P3, K3, rep from * to last 3 (4: 4: 5: 2: 3) sts, P3 (4: 4: 5: 2: 3).

Row 12: K3 (4: 4: 5: 2: 3), P3, *K3, P3, rep from * to last 3 (4: 4: 5: 2: 3) sts, K3 (4: 4: 5: 2: 3).

Row 13: As row 11.

Row 14: K3 (4: 4: 5: 2: 3), P3tog, *K3, P3tog, rep from * to last 3 (4: 4: 5: 2: 3) sts, K3 (4: 4: 5: 2: 3).

Rows 15 and 16: As rows 7 and 8.

These 16 rows complete border.

Beg and ending rows as indicated and repeating the 54 row patt rep throughout, now work in patt from chart as folls:

Inc 1 st at each end of 3rd and every foll 18th (16th: 16th: 14th: 14th: 12th) row to 65 (75: 71: 77: 79: 81) sts, then on every foll 20th (-: 18th: 16th: 16th: 14th) row until there are 71 (-: 75: 79: 81: 85) sts, taking inc sts into patt.

Work 15 rows, ending after patt row 6 (6: 10: 10: 10: 10) and with a WS row.

Shape top

Keeping patt correct, cast off 3 (4: 4: 5: 5: 6) sts at beg of next 2 rows.

65 (67: 67: 69: 71: 73) sts.

Dec 1 st at each end of next 3 rows, then on foll alt row, then on foll 4th row, then on 4 foll 6th rows.

47 (49: 49: 51: 53: 55) sts.

Work 3 rows, ending with a WS row.

Dec 1 st at each end of next and foll 4th row, then on every foll alt row to 39 sts, then on foll 5 rows, ending with a WS row.

Cast off rem 29 sts.

MAKING UP

Press all pieces with a warm iron over a damp cloth.

Join both shoulder seams using back stitch or mattress stitch if preferred.

Neckband

With RS facing and using 2¾mm (US 2) needles, slip 12 (13: 13: 13: 13: 13) sts from right front holder onto right needle, rejoin yarn and pick up and knit 25 (25: 25: 29: 29: 29) sts up right side of neck, 35 (37: 37: 39: 39: 39) sts from back, and 25 (25: 25: 29: 29: 29) sts down left side of neck, then patt across 12 (13: 13: 13: 13: 13) sts on left front holder. 109 (113: 113: 123: 123: 123) sts.

Work in g st for 4 rows, making 9th buttonhole in 2nd of these rows and ending with a RS row. Cast off knitwise (on WS).

Join side seams. Join sleeve seams. Insert sleeves. Sew on buttons.

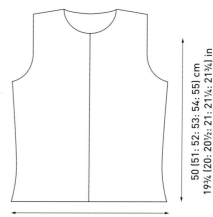

40.5 (43: 45: 48: 50.5: 54.5) cm
16 (17: 17¾: 19: 20: 21½) in

50 (51: 52: 53: 54: 55) cm
19¾ (20: 20½: 21: 21¼: 21¾) in

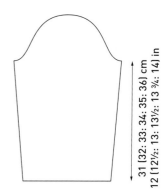

31 (32: 33: 34: 35: 36) cm
12 (12½: 13: 13½: 13 ¾: 14) in

Recommendation

Suitable for the knitter with a little experience
Please see page 46 for photograph.

	XS	S	M	L	XL	XXL	
To fit	**81**	**86**	**91**	**97**	**102**	**109**	**cm**
bust	32	34	36	38	40	43	in

Rowan Fine Milk Cotton

| | 4 | 4 | 5 | 5 | 6 | 6 | x50gm |

Photographed in Opaque

Needles

1 pair 2¼mm (no 13) (US 1) needles
1 pair 2¾mm (no 12) (US 2) needles

Buttons – 10 (10: 10: 10: 11: 11)

Tension

29 sts and 38 rows to 10 cm measured over
stocking stitch using 2¾mm (US 2) needles.

BEL

Neat cropped raglan cardigan

BACK

Cast on 100 (108: 116: 122: 130: 142) sts
using 2¼mm (US 1) needles.
Row 1 (RS): P1 (1: 1: 0: 0: 2), *K2, P2, rep
from * to last 3 (3: 3: 2: 2: 0) sts, K2 (2: 2:
2: 2: 0), P1 (1: 1: 0: 0: 0).
Row 2: K1 (1: 1: 0: 0: 2), *P2, K2, rep from
* to last 3 (3: 3: 2: 2: 0) sts, P2 (2: 2: 2: 2: 0),
K1 (1: 1: 0: 0: 0).
These 2 rows form rib.
Work in rib for a further 20 rows, ending
with a WS row.
Change to 2¾mm (US 2) needles.
Cont in rib, inc 1 st at each end of 17th row.
102 (110: 118: 124: 132: 144) sts.
Work a further 15 rows in rib, ending with
a WS row.
Next row (RS): K3, M1, K to last 3 sts, M1, K3.
104 (112: 120: 126: 134: 146) sts.
Beg with a P row and working all increases as
set by last row, work in st st, shaping side seams
by inc 1 st at each end of 10th and 2 foll 8th
rows. 110 (118: 126: 132: 140: 152) sts.
Work 9 (9: 13: 13: 13: 13) rows, ending with
a WS row.
(Back should measure approx 23 (23: 24: 24:
24: 24) cm.)
Shape raglan armholes
Cast off 5 sts at beg of next 2 rows.
100 (108: 116: 122: 130: 142) sts.
Size XXL only
Next row (RS): K1, K2tog, K to last 3 sts,
K2tog tbl, K1.
Next row: P1, P2tog tbl, P to last 3 sts,
P2tog, P1.
Rep last 2 rows twice more. 130 sts.
All sizes
Work 2 (2: 2: 2: 2: 0) rows, ending with a WS row.
Next row (RS): K1, K2tog, K to last 3 sts,
K2tog tbl, K1.
Working all raglan armhole decreases as set
by last row, dec 1 st at each end of 4th (4th:
4th: 4th: 2nd: 2nd) and 6 (5: 1: 1: 0: 0) foll
4th rows, then on foll 10 (14: 22: 24: 29: 29)
alt rows. 64 (66: 66: 68: 68: 68) sts.
Work 1 row, ending with a WS row. Cast off.

LEFT FRONT

Cast on 56 (60: 64: 67: 71: 77) sts using
2¼mm (US 1) needles.

Row 1 (RS): P1 (1: 1: 0: 0: 2), *K2, P2, rep
from * to last 7 sts, P7.
Row 2: K9, *P2, K2, rep from * to last 3 (3: 3:
2: 2: 0) sts, P2 (2: 2: 2: 2: 0), K1 (1: 1: 0: 0: 0).
Row 3: P1 (1: 1: 0: 0: 2), *K2, P2, rep from *
to last 7 sts, K7.
Row 4: P7, K2, *P2, K2, rep from * to last 3 (3: 3:
2: 2: 0) sts, P2 (2: 2: 2: 2: 0), K1 (1: 1: 0: 0: 0).
These 4 rows set the sts - front opening edge
7 sts in ridge patt and all other sts in rib.
Cont as set for a further 18 rows, ending with
a WS row.
Change to 2¾mm (US 2) needles.
Cont as set, inc 1 st at beg of 17th row.
57 (61: 65: 68: 72: 78) sts.
Work a further 15 rows, ending with a WS row.
Next row (RS): K3, M1, K to last 7 sts, patt 7 sts.
58 (62: 66: 69: 73: 79) sts.
Beg with a P row, working all increases as set
by last row and keeping front opening edge
7 sts in ridge patt throughout, now work rem
sts in st st, shaping side seam by inc 1 st at
beg of 10th and 2 foll 8th rows.
61 (65: 69: 72: 76: 82) sts.
Work 9 (9: 13: 13: 13: 13) rows, ending with
a WS row.
(Left front should measure approx 23 (23: 24:
24: 24: 24) cm.)
Shape raglan armhole
Keeping sts correct, cast off 5 sts at beg
of next row. 56 (60: 64: 67: 71: 77) sts.
Work 3 (3: 3: 3: 3: 1) rows.
Working all raglan armhole decreases as given
for back raglan armhole, dec 1 st at raglan
armhole edge of next 1 (1: 1: 1: 1: 7) rows,
then on 3 (4: 2: 2: 0: 0) foll 4th rows, then
on foll 0 (0: 4: 4: 10: 10) alt rows.
52 (55: 57: 60: 60: 60) sts.
Work 1 row, ending with a WS row.
Shape front neck
Next row (RS): (K1, K2tog) 0 (0: 1: 1: 1: 1)
times, K to last 34 (35: 35: 34: 34: 34) sts
and turn, leaving rem sts on a holder.
18 (20: 21: 25: 25: 25) sts.
Dec 1 st at neck edge of next 8 rows, then on
foll 3 (3: 3: 5: 5: 5) alt rows **and at same time**
dec 1 st at raglan armhole edge of 2nd and
3 (1: 0: 0: 0: 0) foll 4th rows, then on foll
0 (4: 6: 8: 8: 8) alt rows. 3 sts.
Work 1 row, ending with a WS row.

Next row (RS): sl 1, K2tog, psso.
Next row: P1 and fasten off.

RIGHT FRONT

Cast on 56 (60: 64: 67: 71: 77) sts using 2¼mm (US 1) needles.
Row 1 (RS): P9, *K2, P2, rep from * to last 3 (3: 3: 2: 2: 0) sts, K2 (2: 2: 2: 2: 0), P1 (1: 1: 0: 0: 0).
Row 2: K1 (1: 1: 0: 0: 2), *P2, K2, rep from * to last 7 sts, K7.
Row 3: (K3, K2tog, yfwd - to make a buttonhole) 1 (0: 0: 0: 1: 0) times, K2 (7: 7: 7: 2: 7), P2, *K2, P2, rep from * to last 3 (3: 3: 2: 2: 0) sts, K2 (2: 2: 2: 2: 0), P1 (1: 1: 0: 0: 0).
Row 4: K1 (1: 1: 0: 0: 2), *P2, K2, rep from * to last 7 sts, P7.
These 4 rows set the sts - front opening edge 7 sts in ridge patt and all other sts in rib.
Cont as set for 10 (2: 6: 6: 10: 2) rows, ending with a WS row.
Next row (RS): K3, K2tog, yfwd (to make a buttonhole), patt to end.
Working a further 7 (8: 8: 8: 8: 9) buttonholes in this way on every foll 12th row and noting that no further reference will be made to buttonholes, cont as folls:
Cont as set for a further 7 (15: 11: 11: 7: 15) rows, ending with a WS row.
Change to 2¾mm (US 2) needles.
Cont as set, inc 1 st at end of 17th row.
57 (61: 65: 68: 72: 78) sts.
Work a further 15 rows, ending with a WS row.
Next row (RS): Patt 7 sts, K to last 3 sts, M1, K3. 58 (62: 66: 69: 73: 79) sts.
Beg with a P row, working all increases as set by last row and keeping front opening edge 7 sts in ridge patt throughout, now work rem sts in st st, shaping side seam by inc 1 st at end of 10th and 2 foll 8th rows.
61 (65: 69: 72: 76: 82) sts.
Work 10 (10: 14: 14: 14: 14) rows, ending with a **RS** row.
(Right front should measure approx 23 (23: 24: 24: 24: 24) cm.)

Shape raglan armhole

Keeping sts correct, cast off 5 sts at beg of next row.
56 (60: 64: 67: 71: 77) sts.
Work 2 (2: 2: 2: 2: 0) rows.
Working all raglan armhole decreases as given for back raglan armhole, dec 1 st at raglan armhole edge of next 1 (1: 1: 1: 1: 7) rows, then on 3 (4: 2: 2: 0: 0) foll 4th rows, then on foll 0 (0: 4: 4: 10: 10) alt rows.
52 (55: 57: 60: 60: 60) sts.
Work 1 row, ending with a WS row. (9 rows have been worked after 9th (9th: 9th: 9th: 10th: 10th) buttonhole row.)

Shape front neck

Next row (RS): Patt 34 (35: 35: 34: 34: 34) sts and slip these sts onto a holder, K to last 0 (0: 3: 3: 3: 3) sts, (K2tog tbl, K1) 0 (0: 1: 1: 1: 1) times.
18 (20: 21: 25: 25: 25) sts.
Dec 1 st at neck edge of next 8 rows, then on foll 3 (3: 3: 5: 5: 5) alt rows **and at same time** dec 1 st at raglan armhole edge of 2nd and 3 (1: 0: 0: 0: 0) foll 4th rows, then on foll 0 (4: 6: 8: 8: 8) alt rows. 3 sts.
Work 1 row, ending with a WS row.
Next row (RS): sl 1, K2tog, psso.
Next row: P1 and fasten off.

SLEEVES (both alike)

Cast on 76 (78: 80: 82: 84: 88) sts using 2¼mm (US 1) needles.
Row 1 (RS): K0 (0: 1: 0: 0: 1), P1 (2: 2: 0: 1: 2), *K2, P2, rep from * to last 3 (0: 1: 2: 3: 1) sts, K2 (0: 1: 2: 2: 1), P1 (0: 0: 0: 1: 0).
Row 2: P0 (0: 1: 0: 0: 1), K1 (2: 2: 0: 1: 2), *P2, K2, rep from * to last 3 (0: 1: 2: 3: 1) sts, P2 (0: 1: 2: 2: 1), K1 (0: 0: 0: 1: 0).
These 2 rows form rib.
Cont in rib, inc 1 st at each end of 3rd row.
78 (80: 82: 84: 86: 90) sts.
Work 3 (5: 5: 5: 5: 5) rows, ending with a WS row.
Change to 2¾mm (US 2) needles.
Cont in rib, inc 1 st at each end of next and 0 (0: 0: 1: 1: 1) foll 6th row. 80 (82: 84: 88: 90: 94) sts.
Work a further 3 (5: 5: 3: 3: 7) rows in rib, ending with a WS row.

Shape raglan

Keeping rib correct, cast off 5 sts at beg of next 2 rows. 70 (72: 74: 78: 80: 84) sts.
Work 2 rows, ending with a WS row.
Beg with a K row and working all raglan decreases in same way as raglan armhole decreases, now work in st st, dec 1 st at each end of next and 7 (8: 7: 7: 8: 8) foll 4th rows, then on foll 1 (1: 3: 5: 5: 7) alt rows. 52 sts.
Work 1 row, ending with a WS row.

Left sleeve only

Dec 1 st at each end of next row, then cast off 5 sts at beg of foll row. 45 sts.
Dec 1 st at beg of next row, then cast off 5 sts at beg of foll row. 39 sts.
Dec 1 st at beg of next row, then cast off 4 sts at beg of foll row. 34 sts.

Right sleeve only

Cast off 6 sts at beg and dec 1 st at end of next row. 45 sts.
Work 1 row.
Cast off 5 sts at beg and dec 1 st at end of next row. 39 sts.
Work 1 row.
Cast off 4 sts at beg and dec 1 st at end of next row. 34 sts.
Work 1 row.

Both sleeves

Rep last 2 rows 6 times more.
Cast off rem 4 sts.

MAKING UP

Press all pieces with a warm iron over a damp cloth.
Join all raglan seams using back stitch or mattress stitch if preferred.

Neckband

With RS facing and using 2¼mm (US 1) needles, slip 34 (35: 35: 34: 34: 34) sts from right front holder onto right needle, rejoin yarn and pick up and knit 16 (16: 16: 20: 20: 20) sts up right side of neck, 41 sts from top of right sleeve, 62 (64: 64: 66: 66: 66) sts from back, 41 sts from top of left sleeve, and 16 (16: 16: 20: 20: 20) sts down left side of neck, then patt across 34 (35: 35: 34: 34: 34) sts on left front holder. 244 (248: 248: 256: 256: 256) sts.
Row 1 (WS): Patt 7 sts, *K2, P2, rep from * to last 9 sts, K2, patt 7 sts.
Row 2: K3, K2tog, yfwd (to make last buttonhole), K2, *P2, K2, rep from * to last 9 sts, P2, patt 7 sts.
These 2 rows set the sts - front opening edge 7 sts still in ridge patt with all other sts in rib.
Cont as set for a further 3 rows, ending with a WS row.
Cast off in patt.
Join side and sleeve seams. Sew on buttons.

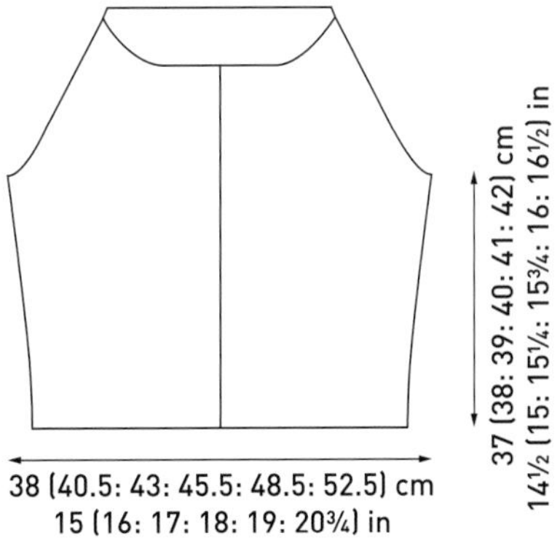
38 (40.5: 43: 45.5: 48.5: 52.5) cm
15 (16: 17: 18: 19: 20¾) in
37 (38: 39: 40: 41: 42) cm
14½ (15: 15¼: 15¾: 16: 16½) in

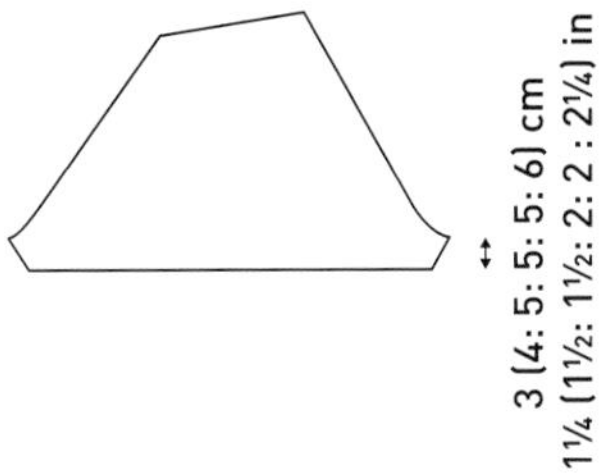
3 (4: 5: 5: 5: 6) cm
1¼ (1½: 1½: 2: 2 : 2¼) in

INFORMATION

A guide to assist with techniques & finishing touches

TENSION

Achieving the correct tension has to be one of the most important elements in producing a beautiful, well fitting knitted garment. The tension controls the size and shape of your finished piece and any variation to either stitches or rows, however slight, will affect your work and change the fit completely.
To avoid any disappointment, we would always recommend that you knit a tension square in the yarn and stitch given in the pattern, working perhaps four or five more stitches and rows than those given in the tension note.

When counting the tension, place your knitting on a flat surface and mark out a 10cm square with pins. Count the stitches between the pins. If you have too many stitches to 10cm your knitting it too tight, try again using thicker needles, if you have too few stitches to 10cm your knitting is too loose, so try again using finer needles. Please note, if you are unable to achieve the correct stitches and rows required, the stitches are more crucial as many patterns are knitted to length.
Keep an eye on your tension during knitting, especially if you're going back to work which has been put to one side for any length of time.

SIZING

The instructions are given for the smallest size. Where they vary, work the figures in brackets for the larger sizes. One set of figures refers to all sizes. The size diagram with each pattern will help you decide which size to knit. The measurements given on the size diagram are the actual size your garment should be when completed.
Measurements will vary from design to design because the necessary ease allowances have been made in each pattern to give your garment the correct fit, i.e. a loose fitting garment will be several cm wider than a neat fitted one, a snug fitting garment may have no ease at all.

WRAP STITCH

A wrap stitch is used to eliminate the hole created when using the short row shaping method. Work to the position on the row indicated in the pattern, wrap the next st (by slipping next st onto right needle, taking yarn to opposite side of work between needles and then slipping same st back onto left needle – on foll rows, K tog the loop and the wrapped st) and turn, cont from pattern.

CHART NOTE

Some of our patterns include a chart. Each square on a chart represent a stitch and each line of squares a row of knitting.

When working from a chart, unless otherwise stated, read odd rows (RS) from right to left and even rows (WS) from left to right. The key alongside each chart indicates how each stitch is worked.

BUTTON FRAMES

Using the amount of strands suggested in the pattern, cover the button frames as indicated in the diagram below or as the recommended by the manufacturer

WORKING A LACE PATTERN

When working a lace pattern it is important to remember that if you are unable to work a full repeat i.e. both the increase and corresponding decrease and vice versa, the stitches should be worked in stocking stitch
or an alternative stitch suggested in the pattern.

FINISHING INSTRUCTIONS

It is the pressing and finishing which will transform your knitted pieces into a garment to be proud of.

Pressing

Darn in ends neatly along the selvage edge. Follow closely any special instructions given on the pattern or ball band and always take great care not to over press your work.
Block out your knitting on a pressing or ironing board, easing into shape, and unless otherwise states, press each piece using a warm iron over a damp cloth.

Tip: Attention should be given to ribs/edgings; if the garment is close fitting – steam the ribs gently so that the stitches fill out but stay elastic. Alternatively if the garment is to hang straight then steam out to the correct shape.

Tip: Take special care to press the selvages, as this will make sewing up both easier and neater.

CONSTRUCTION
Stitching together

When stitching the pieces together, remember to match areas of pattern very carefully where they meet. Use a stitch such as back stitch or mattress stitch for all main knitting seams and join all ribs and neckband with mattress stitch, unless otherwise stated.

Take extra care when stitching the edgings and collars around the back neck of a garment. They control the width of the back neck, and if too wide the garment will be ill fitting and drop off the shoulder.
Knit back neck edgings only to the length stated in the pattern, even stretching it slightly if for example, you are working in garter or horizontal rib stitch.
Stitch edgings/collars firmly into place using a back stitch seam, easing-in the back neck to fit the collar/edging rather than stretching the collar/edging to fit the back neck.

CARE INSTRUCTIONS

Yarns

Follow the care instructions printed on each individual ball band. Where different yarns are used in the same garment, follow the care instructions for the more delicate one.

Buttons

We recommend that buttons are removed if your garment is to be machine washed.

CROCHET

We are aware that crochet terminology varies from country to country. Please note we have used the English style in this publication.

Crochet abbreviations

ch	chain
ss	slip stitch
dc	double crochet
tr	treble
dc2tog	2 dc tog
tr2tog	2 tr tog
yoh	yarn over hook

Double crochet

1. Insert the hook into the work (as indicated in the pattern), wrap the yarn over the hook and draw the yarn through the work only.
2. Wrap the yarn again and draw the yarn through both loops on the hook.
3. 1 dc made

Treble

1. Wrap the yarn over the hook and insert the hook into the work (as indicated on the pattern).
2. Wrap the yarn over the hook draw through the work only and wrap the yarn again.
3. Draw through the first 2 loops only and wrap the yarn again.
4. Draw through the last 2 loops on the hook.
5. 1 treble made.

ABBREVIATIONS

K	knit
P	purl
K1b	knit 1 through back loop
st(s)	stitch(es)
inc	increas(e)(ing)
dec	decreas(e)(ing)
st st	stocking stitch (1 row K, 1 row P)
garter st	garter stitch (K every row)
beg	begin(ning)
foll	following
rem	remain(ing)
rev st st	reverse stocking stitch (1 row P, 1 row K)
rep	repeat
alt	alternate
cont	continue
patt	pattern
tog	together
mm	millimetres
cm	centimetres
in(s)	inch(es)
RS	right side
WS	wrong side
sl 1	slip one stitch
psso	pass slipped stitch over
tbl	through back of loop
M1	make one stitch by picking up horizontal loop before next stitch and knitting into back of it
M1p	make one stitch by picking up horizontal loop before next stitch and purling into back of it
yfwd	yarn forward
yon	yarn over needle
yrn	yarn round needle
MP	Make picot: Cast on 1 st, by inserting the right needle between the first and second stitch on left needle, take yarn round needle, bring loop through and place on left (one stitch cast on), cast off 1 st, by knitting first the loop and then the next stitch, pass the first stitch over the second (one stitch cast off).
Cn	cable needle
C4B	Cable 4 back: Slip next 2 sts onto a cn and hold at back of work, K2, K2 from cn.
C4F	Cable 4 front: Slip next 2 sts onto a cn and hold at front of work, K2, K2 from cn.

THANK YOU!

As always our gratitude goes to our team of fabulous people without whose contributions this book would not be achieved. To Graham for his fantastic work on both the photography and editorial design, Angela for her skills on the page layouts, our most beautiful model Kristie, and Diana for her hair & make-up talents, Sue and Tricia for their pattern writing & checking expertise, our lovely knitters, Ella, Sandra, Margaret & Glennis, and Susan for finishing the garments so well. Also John & the team at Be Authentic, www.beauthentic.co.uk, Holme Valley Scouts, and finally Kate, David, Ann & the Rowan team for their constant support.

Kim, Kathleen & Lindsay

INDEX